INSIGHT COMPACT GUIDE

Norway

Compact Guide: Norway is the ultimate quick-reference guide to this popular Scandinavian destination. It tells you everything you need to know about the country's attractions, from its impressive fjords to its spectacular mountains, from the bright lights of Oslo to the picturesque timbered fishing towns, backed up with detailed information on outdoor activities and events.

This is one of 130 Compact Guides produced by the editors of Insight Guides, whose books have set the standard for visual travel guides since 1970. Packed with information, arranged in easy-to-follow routes, and lavishly illustrated with photographs, this book not only steers you round Norway but also gives you fascinating insights into local life.

APA PUBLICATIONS
Part of the Langenscheidt Publishing Group

Insight Compact Guide: Norway

Written by: Jens-Uwe Kumpch
English version by: Paul Fletcher
Photography by: Blaine Harrington, Gerold Jung, Kim Naylor, Hans Klüche, David Pugh, Jens-Uwe Kumpch
Additional photography by: Fjord Norway: P. Nybø, F. Loftesnes, D. Myrestrand, P. Eide, O. Roksvåg, Ø. Leven, I. Ege, K. H. Olsen, O. I. Worsøe, S. Aske, P. Jonsson, P. Eriksson, O. Apneseth, A. Opdahl, O. J. Grann, O. Johansen, H. Vatne, Herheim Foto, T. Dugstad, Hatlehols, G. Wangen, S. G. Hauge, O. Skjermo, Norwegian State Railways.
Others: Norwegian Tourist Board, Grimstad Turistkontor, Skein Turistkontor, Olympia Utvikling, Top of Europe Norway AS, Destination Sørlandet, Rute 40, Fjordhytter, W. Haraldsen, Rjukan Turistkontor, Turistinformasjonen Molde.
Cover photography by: Robert Harding Picture Library
Design: Roger Williams
Picture Editor: Hilary Genin
Maps: Polyglott/Huber/Maria Randell

Editorial Director: Brian Bell
Managing Editor: Maria Lord
Updater: Daniel Cash

CONTACTING THE EDITORS: As every effort is made to provide accurate information in this publication, we would appreciate it if readers would call our attention to any errors and omissions by contacting:
Apa Publications, PO Box 7910, London SE1 1WE, England
Fax: (44 20) 7403 0290
e-mail: insight@apaguide.co.uk
Information has been obtained from sources believed to be reliable, but its accuracy and completeness, and the opinions based thereon, are not guaranteed.

© 2008 APA Publications GmbH & Co. Verlag KG Singapore Branch, Singapore.
First Edition 1997. Second Edition (Updated) 2007, Reprinted 2008
Printed in Singapore by Insight Print Services (Pte) Ltd
Original edition © Polyglott-Verlag Dr Bolte KG, Munich

Worldwide distribution enquiries:
APA Publications GmbH & Co. Verlag KG (Singapore Branch)
38 Joo Koon Road, Singapore 628990
Tel: (65) 6865-1600, Fax: (65) 6861-6438
Distributed in the UK & Ireland by:
GeoCenter International Ltd
Meridian House, Churchill Way West Basingstoke, Hampshire RG21 6YR
Tel: (44 1256) 817987, Fax: (44 1256) 817988

Distributed in the United States by:
Langenscheidt Publishers, Inc.
36–36 33rd Street 4th Floor, Long Island City, NY 11106
Tel: (1 718) 784-0055, Fax: (1 718) 784-0640

www.insightguides.com

Introduction

Places

Culture

Travel Tips

▽ **Oslo (p22)**
Norway's capital is a
clean and elegant city,
with excellent museums.

◁ **Voringfossen (p73)**
In a land of waterfalls,
this is one of the most
spectacular.

▽ **Vesterålen and
Lofoten Islands (p87)**
Rising straight from
the sea, the huge cliffs
of these islands number
among the great sights
of Norway.

△ **Sognefjord (p49)**
At 200 km (120 miles) lo
and 1,300 metres (4,260
deep, this is the largest of
Norway's dramatic fjords

△ **Bergen (p30)**
quaint wooden buildings
are a special feature of
this old Hansa port.

▽ **Heddal Stave Church (p55)** The largest wooden stave church in the country was built by the 13th century.

△ **Land of Glaciers (p50)** The ice-scapes around Sogn og Fjordane are stunning.

▷ **Telemark (p55)** This region is the home of modern skiing; winter sports of all kinds are very popular in Norway.

◁ **Karasjok (p98)** The main Sami town in the Far North has a museum and theme park of their traditional culture.

▷ **Arctic Ocean Cathedral (p43)** With Europe's largest stained-glass window, the church symbolises the dark winter months and Northern Lights.

A Land of Superlatives

From the spectacular scenery of the west coast to the wilderness of the frozen north and the forests and plains of the southeast, Norway is a country that entices all those in search of unspoilt nature. Cruising on the fjords, driving along spectacular mountain roads, hiking across the vast plateaux, or canoeing on the lakes and among the skerries and islands of the coast are just some of the ways in which the various parts of Norway can be explored. With the aid of a superb transport infrastructure, nothing in the country is too difficult to reach. But it is still possible to enjoy total isolation: 'Summer nights, lonely lakes and never-ending tranquil forests. No sound, no footstep on the paths, my heart was full like dark wine' – the words of Lieutenant Glahn in *Pan* by Norway's 1920 Nobel laureate Knut Hamsun.

Norway's towns were always windows on the world and today, apart from a broad cultural palette, they provide object lessons in the country's long and eventful history: Trondheim, the religious hub of medieval Norway once visited by pilgrims from all over Europe; Bergen, erstwhile capital and historic trading centre and Oslo, today's cosmopolitan capital, representing the aspirations of an independent country that suffered so long under foreign rule.

VIKING BLOOD

Although reconstituted as a country only in 1905 after centuries of domination by Swedes and Danes, Norway can still claim to be the oldest country in Europe: Norwegians can trace an unbroken line of descent to prehistoric times. But it was the Vikings who put Norway on the map. These enterprising Norse men had seafaring skills that enabled them to go out and colonise the then-known world. The old Viking strains still lurk beneath the surface of the Nordic character. The same spirit of adventure propelled Roald Amundsen to discover the South Pole and Thor Heyerdahl to sail his raft, *Kontiki*, across the Pacific.

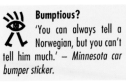

Bumptious?
'You can always tell a Norwegian, but you can't tell him much.' – *Minnesota car bumper sticker.*

Left: Pulpit Rock, Lysefjord
Below: a local girl
Bottom: the Viking tradition

However outgoing the Vikings were, until relatively recently, many rural communities remained extremely isolated. The need for self-sufficiency and survival fostered an independent spirit. Habits were born out of necessity. The easiest way of visiting neighbours in the next valley was not to go round mountains but to ski over the top of them instead. It is therefore no coincidence that Norway became the birthplace of winter sports. The basic transport along and across the deep fjords was by boat, and the Norwegians retain their passion for owning boats today. Scattered communities not only made for an independent spirit but also for great hospitality, and a warm welcome is something at which the Norwegians are still masters.

SITUATION AND LANDSCAPE

Bordered by the Skagerrak, the North Sea, the Atlantic Ocean and the Arctic Ocean, Norway, the western half of the Scandinavian peninsula, runs from the southwest to the northeast like the head and back of a tiger. The southern section is dominated by a huge chain of mountains, the north by the moorland and countless lakes of the vast Finnmark plateau. This is the northernmost point on mainland Europe, extending to the Jan Mayen

Land of fjords...

Islands, Svalbard (Spitzbergen) and Bjørnøya (Bear Island). One-third of the country is north of the Arctic Circle. Oslo, Norway's capital, is 60° N, the same latitude as the Shetland Isles and Cape Labrador, while Hammerfest, the most northerly town in the world, is 10° further north. The north-south coast line measures some 2,600km (1,600 miles).

Norway has an average elevation of 500m (1,640ft). Two-thirds of the country is mountainous, and off its indented coastline lie thousands of islands, holms and skerries. Only 3 percent of the country is arable land. The mountains are a continuation of the Caledonian mountain system of the British Isles, formed in the late Silurian period 400 million years ago from rocks that lay under water. Erosion created impressive landscape features, including numerous peneplains (mountain plateaux), such as the southern Norwegian Hardangervidda (900m/2,950ft), the largest in Europe, covering 11,900 sq km (4,600 sq miles); and the Finnmark plateau at an elevation of about 300m (1,000ft).

But the most stunning feature of the Norwegian landscape is its fjords. These were deep gorges and canyons created along fracture lines in the earth's crust by powerful rivers running westwards to the sea. During the Ice Age of the Quarternary period less than 2½ million years ago, enormous glaciers scoured the valleys and canyons; after the ice had melted, the sea level invaded the valleys and the magnifcent U-shaped fjords were created. Their dramatic effect is enhanced by the valley walls that rise vertically for hundreds of metres, nowhere more impressively than at Pulpit Rock (Prekestolen), which drops vertically 600m (2,000ft) into the Lysefjord. Numerous waterfalls cascading over the edges of the fjords complete the spectacle.

CLIMATE AND WHEN TO GO

The climate, like the landscape, is ever-changing. Variety is the most important characteristic, but some important ground rules apply to both winter and summer. The further north you go, the colder the temperature. In Finnmark it rarely goes

Below: beaches...
Bottom: and glaciers

CLIMATE CHART

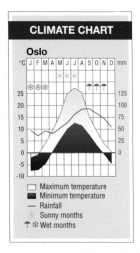

Oslo

- ☐ Maximum temperature
- ■ Minimum temperature
- — Rainfall
- ☀ Sunny months
- ☂☸ Wet months

Månafoss waterfall, Fratfjord

above 20°C (68°F), while in the winter the mercury often drops to –30°C (–22°F); in eastern Finnmark, temperatures sometimes dip to –50°C (–58°F). The seemingly endless western coastline as far as Tromsø is warmed by the Gulf Stream, ensuring that by the coast the annual temperature differences are not as marked as those further inland, and the sea never freezes. However, the rainfall is much greater by the coast. The mountains to the east of the fjords form the watershed and it is here that clouds deposit their rain. The village of Brekke on the south shore of the Sognefjord is one of the wettest places in Europe.

If temperatures between 15 and 25°C (60–77°F) and occasional rain are acceptable, then the time to visit Norway is between May and August. Spring in Norway is short lived. Plants and greenery transform the landscape into a carpet of colour, chasing away the last of the snow, which at higher altitudes, such as on the Hardangervidda, can linger until midsummer day. Summer is the time for campfires on the beach, nights in the open air and fishing trips out to sea. You can get a tan even on northern Norway's sandy beaches but with water temperatures in the region of 12°C (54°F), swimming is not recommended.

For many Norwegians, autumn is the best time of year. Though the season is short, hunters, anglers and walkers head off into the mountains and forests, as the grasses and trees gradually succumb to the cold nights and, as a final gesture, unfold their fantastic array of colours. As darkness closes in, the tranquillity of the forests is broken only by hunters' gunshots.

November to January are for those who just want to ski and the very hardy. The days are short and at high altitudes the temperatures often stay below freezing point all day long.

The skiing season lasts from the start of December to the end of March. As the sun starts to climb, the prepared cross-country tracks through the dense beech forests and across the endless plateaux attract skiers in large numbers. It may seem as though everyone in Norway takes to their skis for the winter or Easter holidays, but cross-country enthusiasts will still enjoy a feeling of solitude as they glide through the countryside. The ski resorts in Hemsedal, Lillehammer and Geilo in the middle of Norway and Narvik in the north all have very good reputations.

FAUNA AND FLORA

The last great Ice Age ended only approximately 5,000 years ago and with a dramatic improvement in the climate, a wide variety of vegetation began to grow in Norway. The tree line rose by several hundred metres, and pines and beech forests covered three-quarters of the Norwegian mountains – ideal conditions for the predators that followed the reindeer, such as wolves and wolverines. In the forests, bears, lynx, pine martens, elks, stags and beavers flourished, but humans were also starting to exploit the woodland.

Below: drying wood
Bottom: cotton grass

Nowadays, approximately 1 million sheep and 200,000 tame reindeer graze on the Norwegian plateaux and hillsides. During the 1950s and '60s, hunters mercilessly pursued the bears, wolverines and lynx, before protective measures were introduced to save their remaining populations. These rare predators have now returned to eastern and northern Norway. The measures to protect elks and beavers have also led to a steady increase in their numbers. With other threatened species, the

age-old conflict between hunter and beast is now controlled by the Environment Ministry.

Norway's coastal islands are inhabited by millions of birds, such as puffins, guillemots, kittiwakes, fulmars, auks and cormorants. Circling sea eagles are a fairly common sight, and on Lofoten and Vesterålen, you will not need binoculars to watch these majestic creatures. In recent winters, the snowy owl has been observed in the Saltfjell mountains and on the Hardangervidda.

The plateaux, which are only clear of snow for around six weeks of the year, do not make ideal habitats for plants and wildlife. Nevertheless, observant walkers may be surprised by the wide range of Arctic flora that they might spot en route. In the Saltfjell mountains north of the Arctic Circle, for example, the limestone rock provides the perfect habitat for a rare species of wild rhododendron that flourishes amid huge fields of white *dryas octopetala* during the short summer.

The higher up and the further north you go, the more sensitive nature is to environmental changes, and great care is taken to protect areas of particular beauty or natural interest. In 1962 the first national park was opened in the Rondane mountains east of Gudbrandsdalen. Now, some 25 national parks in Norway cover an area of more than 23,000 sq km (8,880 sq miles) and there are many other nature reserves.

Below: an Arctic fox and (bottom) reindeer

POPULATION

Including the inhabited Svalbard Islands and Norway's population is just over 4.6 million – approximately 12 people per square kilometre. Many regions are uninhabitable mountain areas, but there is still a great deal of room for everyone. The bulk of the population is concentrated on the southern and western coasts, where most of the towns are situated. In and around Oslo, Bergen, Stavanger and Trondheim, population density matches any other European city. The vast tracts of country to the north of Trondheim, by contrast, are occupied by only 14 percent of the population. In the Finnmark region in the far north, some settlements lie as far as 100km (60 miles) apart.

One result of this clear north-south divide is the 'District Policy', under which generous tax benefits are granted to those living in the north. In the thinly populated areas, the contribution to Gross Domestic Product is relatively high, due to tourism and fishing. The aim of the government's District Policy is to keep the economic and population structure intact and to prevent a southward migration.

RELIGION

Around 75 percent of all Norwegians belong to the Evangelical Lutheran National Church, which is endowed by the government. Other religious groups include Pentecostalists, the Lutheran Free Church, Roman Catholics, Methodists, Baptists, Muslims, Buddhists and Islamic denominations. However, it would be wrong to conclude that the majority of Norwegians are devout Christians – only around 3 percent are regular church-goers.

LANGUAGE

Officially, there are two written languages in Norway: Bokmål (a modified version of standard Danish) and Nynorsk (a composite language of the many local dialects). For over 80 percent of school children, Bokmål is the main language. However, while outsiders will probably be hard-pressed to tell the difference between the two, it

> **Norwegian trolls**
> Among the many folk tales of Norway, those of the trolls are the most enduring. These near-human creatures live in among the forests and mountains and only come out after the sun has gone down. They can be spiteful, are easily roused and can transform themselves into other manifestations at will. Many places in Norway are associated with trolls and their tales. The folkloric figures make memorable souvenirs.

A typical troll

> **The singing Sami**
> Sami have a particular way of singing called 'joiking' in which words are islolated and sub-ordinated to the rhythm and melody. This probably developed as a way of quitening reindeer while keeping wild animals at bay, and young men used to compose them for the girls they courted. For centuries the Church tried to outlaw it, but today 'joiking' is still popular, and a 'joik' may be composed for any occasion.

is of great importance to many Norwegians that they speak 'their' language. Countless dialects are still in use, and the choice of the right language is always a matter for lively debate.

THE SAMI PEOPLE

The Sami people, or 'Lapps', have lived in northern Scandinavia for more than 8,000 years. Latest estimates put their numbers at around 70,000; about 40,000 of them live on Norwegian soil, mostly in Finnmark, the country's northernmost county.

Like many other people living in close contact with nature, the Sami were shamanists. From the 12th century, the teachers of Christianity did their best to combat the ancient beliefs; the tribes were converted and churches were built. The Sami did not recognise state boundaries, but grazed their herds of reindeer on the same pastureland that their ancestors had used. In the 18th and 19th century, missionaries promoted the use of Sami language in schools. But from 1902 onwards, it was forbidden to sell land to anyone who could not speak Norwegian. From the Middle Ages until fairly recently, the Sami have been the victims of blatant discrimination. The event which highlighted their grievances occurred in 1980–81, when the Alta River was dammed and large areas of reindeer grazing land were lost.

Nowadays, every Sami is taught the Sami language and, under a new law, the Norwegian government has agreed to do everything in its power to help maintain the Sami language, culture and lifestyle. In 1989, the Sameting or Sami parliament, which is based in Karasjok in Finnmark, was inaugurated with every member directly elected by all Samis. Although the Sameting has limited influence on the Oslo government, the two do at least have to agree on any decisions concerning the Sami.

The main problem facing the community is migration to the cities, but those who stay behind are benefitting from tourism. The best – although also the harshest – time to visit the region of Finnmark is in winter when ice-fishing

Sami in Finnmark

under the Northern Lights or riding on a reindeer sledge are unforgettable experiences.

ECONOMY

Although still very much a country of farmers and fishermen, Norway has been transformed into one of the richest countries in the world. But tourists who visit see hardly anything of the nation's industrial base. There are no nuclear or coal-fired power stations, but high levels of rainfall in the west of the country have been fully exploited and plentiful supplies of hydro-electric power give the country an important competitive advantage in international markets. The use of water for generating electricity is closely linked with the electrochemical and metallurgy industries and the production of aluminium and metal alloys, mainly for motor manufacturers, is one of the main on-shore sources of employment.

At the beginning of the 1960s, the North Sea and the North Atlantic were divided up between Norway, Denmark and Great Britain, and Norway's share of the continental shelf is four times the size of the country. Between 1972 and 1997, oil and gas production volumes steadily increased. Oil production is vulnerable because international oil prices often fluctuate dramatically;

Below and bottom: fishing is still a major industry

gas production, however, is still rising. Some 43 percent of all Norwegian economic activity relies on exports – a dependency that worries the nation's politicians. And Norway steadfastly remains outside the European Union. Its citizens earn good salaries and seem quite satisfied with their social systems. Tourists still feel the high cost of living when travelling in Norway, however.

Below: oil rig worker
Bottom: Oslo's city hall

Norway's economy has boomed thanks to North Sea oil. Only Saudi Arabia and Russia export more oil than Norway, it makes up 45 percent of the country's exports. Norway saves its oil-boosted budget surpluses in a Government Petroleum Fund, which is invested abroad and is valued at more than US$190 billion. However, Norwegians still worry about that time in the next two decades when the oil and gas begin to run out. Fishing continues to be a major industry. Exports are worth about US$3 billion, with modern fish farming methods playing an increasingly important role.

ADMINISTRATION

Norway is a constitutional hereditary monarchy. There is common consensus among political parties that the country needs a king – with no great political power, but vested with almost unlimited trust. Born in 1937, Harald V has been on the throne since 1991.

All legislative and taxation powers lie with the Storting, whose 165 members are elected every four years as representatives of the country's 19 *fylker* (counties). Altogether eight different political parties are represented, ranging from the Progress Party on the right of the spectrum to the Christian Democratic Party and the Socialist Left Party. A Norwegian sociologist once claimed that in Norway all the political parties are only variations on the Social Democratic Party, which has ruled Norway for longer than any other party since the 1930s.

It was only in 1997 that the socialist rule came to an end when Kjell Magne Bondevik, a Christian Democrat, became prime minister in a centre-right coalition. In 2000, Jens Stoltenberg of the Labour Party briefly became the new prime minister and the following year Mr Bondevik once more picked up the reins of power, with a newly formed coalition government. In 2005, Stoltenberg's Labour Party led a three-party coalition to win the general election.

Almost as many women as men sit in the Storting. Norway was the first European country to give women the vote, in 1913. Since then many women have attained ministerial positions, including Dr Gro Harlem Brundtland, who was prime minister for many years, until she resigned in 1996. She subsequently took a position as Director-General in Geneva with the World Health Organisation.

Much is written about Scandinavian-style social democracy. The state still provides for its citizens' health and pensions, and unemployment insurance is financed through taxation. Norwegian taxes may seem high, but the state is by far the biggest employer in the country. However, in times of growing unemployment and unpredictable oil revenues, less is spent on education and job-creation schemes.

After a second referendum in 2001, voters decided by 52 percent to 48 percent against membership of the EU. The Union's rules and regulations were of concern to farmers and fishermen who rely on heavy government protection. Many other Norwegians felt pride in what they see as a young country, and wanted to maintain the independent status it had won in 1905.

Drinks on the state

Vinmonopolet was created in 1922 as a shareholders' company to monopolise and regulate the sale of alcohol, which has long been a contentious issue in the country. Vinmonopolet shops remain the only places where you can buy alcohol (including beer with more than 4.75 percent alcohol), which is very expensive, and a principal source of tax revenue.

Royal guard, Oslo

HISTORICAL HIGHLIGHTS

12000–2500BC With the recession of the last Ice Age, hunters and fishers move slowly northwards along the west coast. Enormous rock carvings are created around 4,000BC at Alta in Finnmark. Around 5,000BC, dwellings are built in the south of the country.

3000–2500BC New migrants, mostly farmers, settle in eastern Norway, but hunting and fishing remain important.

1500BC onwards Bronze is introduced and used by chieftains for the production of weapons and brooches. Huge burial mounds are built close to the sea. Figurative rock carvings are highly stylised.

1st–5th centuries AD The Norwegians are in contact with Roman-occupied Gaul. The runic alphabet appears in the country in the 3rd century.

6th–9th centuries Chieftains' graves indicate the emergence of petty states based on clans or tribes. Each has its own *ting*, or regional assembly.

800–1050 The Viking Age. The Norwegians raid and settle northeast England, Scotland, Ireland, northern France and Iceland, before advancing further west to Greenland and North America. The Vikings' contact with western Europe is decisive for the unification and Christianisation of Norway.

c 900 The Viking chief Harald Fairhair from the Oslo Fjord pacifies the western coast, unifies the country and proclaims himself king. His son, Erik Bloodaxe, is notorious for having murdered seven of his brothers.

c 950 With the aid of English missionaries, King Håkon the Good, who had been brought up in England, gives the Norwegians their first taste of Christianity. His attempts at mass conversion fail and he dies in battle in 960.

1000 At the Battle of Svold against the Swedish and Danish fleet, the Christian King Olav Tryggvason jumps overboard and is never seen again.

1015 Olav II Haraldsson (later St Olav) is acknowledged as king throughout Norway. He consolidates royal power and continues the Christianisation process, but is killed at Stiklestad in 1030 *(see page 40)*.

1047 After a lurid career as a mercenary with the Varangian Guard, Harald III Hådråde becomes king. He invades England to claim the throne in 1066, but is killed at the battle of Stamford Bridge.

12th century The first Norwegian monasteries and cathedrals are established in the early part of the century. At the same time, kings expand their direct rule over various provinces. In 1153 an archbishopric is established in Nidaros (Trondheim), heralding the start of a power struggle between church and state.

13th century A 'Golden Age' begins under Håkon IV, who overhauls administration and establishes a new law of succession. Under his successor, Magnus VI, royal judges preside over the *ting*. In 1262 Iceland and Greenland accept Norwegian sovereignty, marking the height of the Norwegian empire. In 1266, the Hebrides and the Isle of Man are ceded to Scotland, who recognises the Norwegian claim to the Orkney and Shetland islands.

14th century The Hanseatic League, a commercial association of towns formed to protect and control trade, dominates along the Norwegian coast.

1349 Plague kills half of Norway's population. This causes the abandonment of farms and the decline of many nobles into the peasant class.

1397 Denmark, Sweden and Norway are united under the Danish throne when the heir of Margaret I, Erik of Pomerania, is crowned king in Kalmar, Sweden. Governed from Copenhagen, Norway becomes an increasingly unimportant part of Scandinavia, remaining in a union with Denmark until 1814.

1468 Christian I of Oldenburg pawns the Orkney and Shetland islands to provide a dowry for his daughter.

c 1500 Knut Alvsson leads an uprising to create an independent state but is murdered in Akershus Castle in Oslo.

1536 Norway is proclaimed a Danish province. Danish becomes the official language but the Norwegians keep most of their institutions and laws. In the wake of the Reformation, the Archbishopric of Trondheim is dissolved.

17th century The Danish Christian IV founds towns, including Kristiansand (to control the Skagerrak) and Christiania (after fire destroyed medieval Oslo).

1807–14 In the Napoleonic wars, Denmark-Norway joins the alliance against England. The English blockade brings isolation and economic crisis, convincing leading groups in Norway of the need for political autonomy.

1814 Under the Kiel peace settlement, Norway is ceded to Sweden. With Danish aid, a Norwegian assembly is establish at Eidsvoll north of Oslo. On 17 May, a constitution for an independent Norway is declared. Sweden responds with military force and Norway enters a union with Sweden, with a shared king.

1905 Parliament declares the union with Sweden dissolved. Danish-born Håkon VII becomes king of Norway.

1914–18 Norway neutral in World War I.

1935 Norwegian Workers' Party (DNA) forms a government for the first time.

9 April 1940 The German army attacks Oslo and major ports along the west coast as far as Narvik. King and government flee to London, while the Norwegian resistance movement struggles against the German occupation.

7 May 1945 The Germans capitulate. Retreating from Finland in the winter of 1944–5 they leave scorched earth.

1949 Norway is a founding member of NATO; 10 years later it joins EFTA (European Free Trade Association).

1968 Oil is discovered in the North Sea.

1972 In a referendum, 53.5 percent vote against European Union membership.

1993 International outrage as Norway resumes commercial whaling.

1994 Norway hosts Winter Olympics.

2000 Oslo celebrates its 1,000th year, Bergen is European City of Culture.

2001 A right-wing coalition takes power after the general election, with the support of the far-right Progress Party.

2004 Norway bans smoking in restaurants, bars and cafés.

2005 A left-wing coalition led by the Labour Party wins the general election.

2006 Oslo is named the world's most expensive city.

Map on page 24

Previous page: Geirangerfjord
Below: on the sunny quay at
Aker Brygge
Bottom: the city's wooded hills

1: Oslo

If you arrive in Norway's capital by ferry and have passed the countless islands and holms in the 100-km (60-mile) long Oslofjord, then you will be struck by wooded hills in the background and shores lined with port installations, ferries and commercial vessels in the foreground. Between them lies a town, which has only recently evolved from a dullish 'provincial' capital to a modern cosmopolitan city.

HISTORY

Situated at the end of Norway's most eastern fjord, the trading centre of Oslo developed into a town some time in the 11th century. After being designated capital of the Norwegian empire by King Håkon V (reigned 1299–1319), Oslo was the site where the Norwegian kings were crowned until 1514. In the Hanseatic period, however, its importance as Norway's main port diminished.

After the fire of 1624, Christian IV rebuilt the town and changed its name to Christiania, but it was not until the late 18th and 19th centuries that the settlement grew into a European-style city. The first Norwegian university opened here in 1813; in 1814 it was redesignated the country's capital.

THE MODERN CITY

Oslo's increasing political importance had an impact on the city's subsequent growth. At the beginning of the 20th century, it was Norway's main centre for imports. In 1925, the name Christiania was abandoned in favour of the city's old name – Oslo. In 1948, when the district of Akershus was incorporated into the municipality, Oslo became one of the biggest cities in Europe in terms of surface area, encompassing some 454 sq km (175 sq miles). The 521,000 inhabitants occupy only a quarter of this space. If you were to ask any of the residents what makes the city so attractive, then they will almost certainly reply: Nordmarka. Nordmarka includes the popular skiing area of Holmenkollen, numerous lakes, vast woodland and seemingly endless footpaths that would take days to cover. Set in a broad valley, the city also has a favourable micro-climate.

Star Attraction
● Akershus

Getting around easily
The easiest way to travel round the city is to invest in an Oslokortet (Oslo Card), available from tourist offices, most hotels and some newsagents. It is a city-wide travel pass for buses, trains and ferries and gives discounts on boat and coach sightseeing tours. It offers free parking in council car parks, and free or reduced entry to museums and some cinemas. Oslo Cards are valid for one, two or three days.

SIGHTS

The city centre of Oslo is laid out in a chequerboard pattern and can easily be covered on foot in two to three hours. ★★ **Akershus ❶** (outdoor area open daily, times vary for centre), the huge fortress on the east side of the bay, was built in several stages. It was started by Håkon V Magnusson around 1300, but was transformed into a Renaissance-style palace in the late 16th century by Christian IV.

Within the walls of the Akershus stand the impressive **Norwegian Armed Forces Museum** and the **Resistance Museum**. The national memorial occupies the harbour end of the castle precinct. The palace is used by the Norwegian government for official receptions, and members of the Norwegian royal family are buried in the **Royal Mausoleum**.

The centre of the city gradually moved northwards towards the Central Station, the Storting, the university and the royal palace, leaving intact a number of houses from the Christiania period in the part of the city between the station and the

Akershus

Map
below

Akershus. Interesting relics from the days before the nation was founded include the 17th-century ★ **Stattholdergården** restaurant and the ★ **Mustadgården**, both of which retain their original dimensions. By the Rådhusgata, notable buildings include Oslo's oldest ★ **Town Hall** (1641), now a top-class restaurant, and the ★ **Rådhuset** (city hall) ❷, a landmark that dominates the harbour area. It took 17 years to complete and, after opening in 1950, it now houses the city administration offices. The tourist office is located just nearby, to the north of the City Hall.

★ **Karl Johans gate**, the city's main shopping street, was laid out in 1835. It runs from the sta-

Below: the historic harbour
Bottom: Karl Johans gate

tion to the Royal Palace, and is an embodiment of modern Norway. Throughout the year, it is alive with activity: street theatre, market stalls and crowds of people of all nationalities. The street is also home to a number of brasseries and is a good place to people-watch.

A narrow pedestrianised zone ends by the ★ **Storting ❸**, the Norwegian parliament building which dates from the mid-19th century. After a coffee in the dignified Grand Café in the Grand Hotel, where Ibsen spent many an afternoon, or, if it's sunny, at the open-air Sara's Telt opposite, with lovely views over the fountain, head for the ★★ **National Gallery** (Nasjonal-

Star Attraction
● National Gallery

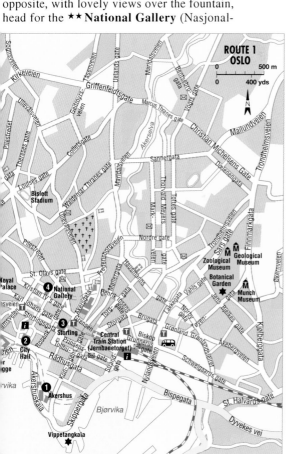

Map on page 24

galleriet, tel: 22 20 04 04) ❹, in Universitetsgata, where the nation's main art treasures are
housed (open Tues, Wed, Fri 10am–6pm, Thur
10am–8pm, Sat–Sun 10am–5pm. Guided tours
in English on Mon, Wed, Fri at 10am, noon and
2pm). As well as two rooms devoted to paintings by Edvard Munch, 4,000 works by other
Norwegian painters are on display.

ROYAL PALACE

Karl Johans gate ends by the ★★ **Royal Palace** ❺
which has a park and huge square. Built between
1824 and 1848, the palace is the home of Harald
V and Queen Sonja and the House of Schleswig-
Holstein-Sonderburg-Glücksburg, and it was
here that wedding celebrations were held for
Crown Prince Haakan and Mette Marit when
they married in 2001. The palace is open to the
public June–mid-Aug (guided tours Mon–Thur
and Sat at 2pm and 2.20pm. Otherwise it's worth
having a stroll in the park for the view over the
city. To the right of the palace, a 10-minute walk
away, lies the port.

The Royal Palace

The harbour area is very popular thanks to the
development around old west station, an exhibition centre, and the ★★ **Aker Brygge** ❻ quay.
On sunny days, this promenade is a delight. Sailing ships moor along the quay, while young and
old sit outside and enjoy a beer or an ice cream
in one of the many cafés and restaurants. On the
other side of the bay, the Akershus fortress stands
proud. On such days Aker Brygge appears to
belong in a more southerly latitude.

To visit the city's best museums, start with a
ferry ride from Rådhusbrygge to the ★★ **Bygdøy**
peninsula, Oslo's most exquisite quarter. The
ferry moors right next to the *Gjøa,* the ship that
was used by Roald Amundsen when he negotiated the Northwest Passage through Canada
between 1903 and 1906.

The ferry leaves from Pier 3 at the back of the
Rådhuset and you get off at Dronningen. You can
also take Bus 30 marked Bygdøy, from the
National Theatre and ask to get off at the Folk

Museum. Lunch or dine at the Lanternen Kro, a traditional inn at Huk Aveny 2.

MARITIME MUSEUM

A stroll through the maritime history of Norway begins at the **Norwegian Maritime Museum ❼** (Norsk Sjøfartsmuseum, Norsk, open summer daily 10am–6pm, Sept–mid-May 10.30am–4pm, Thur until 6pm), the **Fram Museum** (open all year, times vary) and the **Kontiki Museum** (open all year, times vary). Exhibits of Norway's heroic explorers include the *Fram*, the exploration ship used by Nansen and Amundsen, most notably on their Antarctic expedition; the *Kontiki* raft, built in 1947 by Larvik-born Thor Heyerdahl who sailed it from Peru to Polynesia to test his theory that the first Polynesians came from South America; and his papyrus raft *Ra II*, in which he sailed across the Atlantic in 1970.

The three Viking ships exhibited a few minutes' walk away from the polar vessels were in many respects the forerunners of ships commisioned for more modern explorers. *Oseberg, Gokstad* and *Tune* in the ★★★ **Viking Ship Museum** (Vikingskipshuset, Huk Aveny 35, open daily summer 9am–6pm, Oct–Apr 11am–4pm) confirm the remarkable boatbuilding skills of the Norsemen. Platforms enable you to get good views of the hulls.

Star Attractions
● Royal Palace
● Aker Brygge
● Bygdøy
● Viking Ship Museum

Below: Viking Ship Museum
Bottom: Amundsen's 'Fram'

Map on page 24

Below: traditional dress and (bottom) Gol stave church, Norwegian Folk Museum

FOLK MUSEUM

If you have plenty of time to spare, then try to fit in a visit to the ★★ **Norwegian Folk Museum ❽** (Norsk Folkemuseum, Museumsveien 10, tel: 22 12 37 00, open daily summer: 10am–6pm; mid-Sept–mid-May Mon–Fri 11am–3pm, Sat–Sun 11am–4pm). Opened in 1894, it offers a comprehensive insight into the Norwegian way of life from the Reformation to the present day.

Examples of both rural and urban architecture are preserved in this open-air museum, which features 155 reconstructed authentic timber houses. Displays inside include contemporary furniture and household goods and utensils. Probably the most striking medieval building in the open-air section is the **Gol stave church**. Whether your interests lie in the history of Norwegian music, church, medicine or in Sami culture, it's advisable to set aside at least two full days to see all the exhibits. In summer, outdoor activities such as folk dancing and traditional cooking take place.

VIGELANDSPARK

If you want to soak up more Norwegian culture, this time with the emphasis on art and nature, take bus 20 to Frogner Plass and visit the Vigeland Museum (Vigeland-museet, Nobelsgate 32, open Tues–Sun June–Aug 11am–5pm, Sept–May noon–

4pm), named after the Norwegian sculptor Gustav Vigeland (1869–1943), and then on to ★★ **Vigelandspark ❾** (open 24 hours). The park is home to more than 200 monumental sculptures, and makes a good trip just outside the city, particularly during the summer when it is a playground for both young and old. Don't let the rain put you off either – the park is still worth a visit, even in the wet.

From the north of the park it is only 10 minutes' walk to the ★ **International Museum of Children's Art ❿** (Barn e Kunstmuseet Det Internasjonale, tel: 22 46 85 73, open Tues–Thur 9.30am–2pm, Sun 11am–4pm, closed 8 Aug–17 Sept), in Lille Frøens Vei. This modern museum not only displays children's art from more than 180 countries, but allows youngsters to let their imagination run riot in the hope that one day their work will be exhibited here.

SKI JUMP

Now leave the town behind and explore the surrounding area with its villas, woods and footpaths. Nearby Frøen subway station is on the Holmenkollen line; every 15 minutes a train stops here on its way up to Oslo's best-known summit, some 227m (745ft) above sea level.

Do not miss the opportunity to visit the Skiing Museum beneath the ★★ **Holmenkollen Ski Museum and Jump Tower ⓫** (Kongeveien 5, tel: 22 92 32 00, open daily summer 9am–8pm, spring and autumn 10am–5pm, winter 10am–4pm). Try the ski simulator to imagine making the jump, but do make the ascent if only for the view which extends across the city centre and out over the fjord. Oslo is a beautiful city, especially from this perspective. The first ski jump was built in 1892, and has since been modernised and expanded about 15 times.

This recently expanded national ski facility is open throughout the year, with a café and souvenir shop. The museum exhibits the history of skiing over 4,000 years. There are also exhibitions of polar expeditions made by Roald Amundsen and Fridtjof Nansen, and the ski history of the royal family.

Star Attractions
- Norwegian Folk Museum
- Vigelandspark
- Holmenkollen Ski Museum

Vigelandspark sculpture park

Map
on page
31

*Below: Bergenser
marching boy
Bottom: the fish market*

2: Bergen

Norway's second largest city has a population of
230,000, around half the size of the capital; its history as an important Hansa trading port resounds
along its quaint wooden quays. Bergen's pride, traditions and dialect are so strong that Bergensers
often like to think of themselves as a race apart.

To confirm their traditions, every Saturday and
Sunday from mid-March to May all five- to eight-
year-olds march through the town centre of
Bergen. By the time of the grand finale on Independence Day (17 May), they will have learnt
to march in time with a drum and, depending on
their age, to carry either a crossbow or a wooden
rifle; but more importantly, they will have become
proper 'Bergensers'. These youngsters live in the
Vågen harbour district, talk in a local dialect that
is incomprehensible to non-speakers, and will
be eternally proud to have been born here and to
have belonged to the Buekorps. Just as long as
they are marching and the rain continues to fall,
then everything in Bergen is okay. Hardly anywhere else in Europe sees as much rain as Bergen.
There is even an umbrella-repair store in Bergen.
Bergensers like to make jokes about themselves
– the stickers on many of the local cars say: 'I
am not from Norway, I am from Bergen'.

TOWN PLANNING

The houses, churches and residential districts
around the harbour serve as a history lesson.
Despite countless fires, particularly on the north
side of the Vågen, timber continues to be the main
building material. The districts of Sandviken and
Nordnes around the Vågen and the Puddefjord
are architecturally homogeneous and illustrate the
clear boundary between the merchant class and
the mariners and workers.

HISTORY

Bergen has been a maritime town since it was
founded by King Olav Kyrre ('the Peaceful') in

1070. In the 13th and 14th centuries it was not just Norway's capital and religious centre, but also a major harbour for trade with all the islands to the west. Salt and wheat were exchanged for dried fish during the Hanseatic period *(see page 18)*, and business was especially good in the 14th century, when the Hansa established an office here, and all the trade was handled by German merchants. After the Germans were driven out of the city, Bergen continued to be an attractive base for international traders and shipowners. During World War II Bergen became the centre of the Resistance movement. It was chosen as a European City of Culture in 2000.

Ole Bull

The violinist Ole Bull, who founded Bergen's National Theatre in 1850, wandered the villages of west Norway and the Jotundheim mountain plateau to collect old folk melodies. He played them on a Hardanger fiddle, the region's traditional instrument. Edvard Gried later transcribed some of them for piano to prevent them being lost.

ROUTE 2
BERGEN

0   300 m
0   300 yds

N

Skuteviken

Old Bergen Open-Air Museum

Fishery Museum

Bergen-hus

Rosenkranztarnet

Mariakirken ❸

Bryggen Museum ❹ Schøtstuene

❼ Aquarium

Strandgaten

Nordnesvelen

Tollbodalm

Vågen

Bryggen

❷

Hanseatic Museum ❺

Funicular Station

Fløyen ❻

Buekorps Museum

Strandkaien

Strandgaten

❶ Torget (Fish Market)

Town Hall

Leprosy Museum ❽

Railway Station

Puddefjorden

West Norway Museum of Decorative Arts ❾

Fest-plassen

Lille Lunge-gårdsvann

Rasmus Meyer Collection
Stenersen Collection

Grieghalle

University Ⓜ Museum of Natural History

Maritime Museum Ⓜ

Museum of Cultural History Ⓜ Botanical Gardens

Welhavens gate

Map
on page
31

*Below and bottom:
Bryggen's 18th-century
wooden warehouses*

SIGHTS

Measured by turnover, Bergen is one of the largest ports in the world, with the oil reserves in the North Sea playing a major part in its prosperity. Several suburbs on the other side of the seven hills have been incorporated into the municipality, but the central area around the ★★ **Fish Market ❶** at Torget has a small-town look that has changed little since the 19th century. From 7am, when the stalls open to sell fresh cod, pollock, salmon and shrimps, the Bergensers head straight for their regular fishmonger and buy their fish, even though it is no cheaper here than anywhere else. For a taste of old Bergen, dine at the Bryggeloftet & Stuene at Bryggen 11.

Within walking distance of the Fish Market is the **Bergen Museum**, which has cultural and historical material, from prehistoric and medieval times, and an exhibition about the Viking way of life.

★★ **Bryggen ❷**, Bergen's most famous street, is lined with fine wooden warehouses, rebuilt after the great fire of 1702. Bryggen is on UNESCO's World Heritage List. At the far end, to the right, stands the ★**Mariakirken ❸**, a church that dates from the first half of the 12th century and is the oldest building still in use. It is justly proud of its rich baroque pulpit. The only other medieval churches to survive periodic fires are the present **Domkirke**

(cathedral) and **Korskirken** both near the harbour and worth a visit. Next to the Mariakirken are the ★ **Schøtstuene** ❹, the three guildhalls and a kitchen built by the Hanseatic merchants so that they could meet, talk business and drink. In a drawer is the cane used to discipline the apprentices who had their schooling here.

HANSEATIC MUSEUM

The early 18th-century **Hanseatic Museum** ❺ (tel: 55 31 41 89, open daily 9am–5pm in summer, otherwise times vary; guided tours in summer) at the start of Bryggen was once the home and office of a wealthy merchant. A ★ **gallery** in a courtyard at the end of a narrow lane houses the works of the late Audun Hetland, one of Norway's best caricaturists. He liked to poke fun at the relationship between the town's inhabitants and their damp environment.

Bergen's shopping centre is situated on the left-hand side of the bay around the **Torgalmenning**, a broad, traffic-free street where many of the best shops are to be found. Crowded in high summer, these thoroughfares, known as *almenning*, were built wide to prevent flames from spreading to the opposite side of the street.

SPECTACULAR VIEWS

The view from the **Nordnes** peninsula or **St John's Church** over the town centre and across to the popular Fløyen lookout point is characterised by the contrast between the green woodland, the blue sea and the mainly whitewashed wooden houses. If you want an even more striking view, take the scenic tram to the ★★ **Fløyen** ❻ and enjoy the whole vista from the landward side. At the top is the lovely old-fashioned building that houses Fløyen Restaurant, built in 1925, and the start of eight marked walking routes. In the west, the North Sea shimmers beyond the offshore islands while, to the southeast, the snow-covered **Folgefonn glacier** gleams in the bright sunlight – all, of course, weather permitting. Make the most of such sunny days and save

Bergen Card
The Bergen Card provides free bus travel within the city, parking, travel on the scenic tram, and admission to most museums and attractions, with discounts on sightseeing. Cards can be purchased at the tourist office at Vågsallmenningen l, the train station, the express boat terminal, and most hotels.

Special sightseeing tours between 1 May and 30 September include city bus tours, walking tours of Old Bryggen and an hour-long tour by the Bergen Express Train.

View from the Fløyen

Map on page 31

Below: the aquarium
Bottom: Fantoft stave church

a visit to the excellent ★ **Aquarium** ❼ or one of the museums for one of Bergen's many rainy days.

Few people will have heard of Dr Armauer Hansen, but he has been indirectly responsible for saving many lives, having discovered the leprosy bacteria in 1869. The ★ **Leprosy Museum** ❽ in an old hospital recalls his and other doctors' achievements (open in summer 11am–3pm). Art lovers may want to visit the **Rasmus Meyer Collection** (with works by Norwegian artists, including Munch) at the Bergen Art Museum, the **Lysverket** (Norwegian and International art from the 15th century to the present) in the same building, and the **West Norway Museum of Decorative Arts** ❾ (open Tues–Sun 11am–4pm, low season noon–4pm) – all situated on the other side of the Lille Lungegårdsvann lake.

On the north side of the town is **Gamle Bergen** (Old Bergen; open summer only), an open-air museum of 40 wooden buildings from the 18th and 19th centuries, with tour guides in traditional red, calf-length costumes and black shawls. Nearby is the **Sandvik Sjøbad**, a popular swimming area which looks out over Byfjorden to the city.

EXCURSIONS

The ancient ★★ **Fantoft stave church**, built in 1150, was destroyed by arsonists in 1992, but was faithfully restored within three years. It lies around 8km (5 miles) south of Bergen. Buses leave every 20 minutes from the bus station next to the railway station, terminal 20. Fantoft is a 10-minute journey; the church is signposted from the station.

Continue on the bus to **Hopsbroen** and then follow signs to Troldhaugen, a 15-minute walk. ★★ **Troldhaugen** ('Hill of the Trolls'; times vary, tel: 55 92 29 92), a 20-minute walk, was the family home of the composer, Edvard Grieg. When he moved here at the age of 42 in 1885, he was already famous. He stayed until his death in 1907 and the local people have since welcomed many thousands of visitors. You can tour the museum, view the summer house where Grieg worked, see his and his wife Nina's graves, which were hewn out of the rock, and visit the concert hall (1985).

3: Kristiansand

Most visitors to Kristiansand arrive by boat, and those who emerge from the bowels of a car ferry from Denmark will discover a town that has many similarities with the country they left just across the Skagerrak. But Kristiansand is now Norway's Riviera. It lives off its reputation as the country's sailing capital, and the surrounding area enjoys a favoured climate. Amateur sailors navigate around the surrounding tiny rocky islands in the Skagerrak well into October. Spring and summer last longer in Kristiansand than in any other part of Norway.

Star Attractions
● Fantoft stave church
● Troldhaugen

Sailing capital

HISTORY

Kristiansand was founded and fortified by Christian IV in 1641. He encouraged wealthy local farmers to make their homes on the peninsula by the harbour, but there were still only 4,800 inhabitants here in 1800. Initially it was maritime

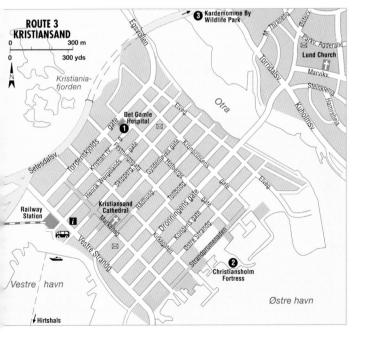

Map on page 35

Skating record
The oldest skating club in the world, Oddersja Skiog Skoytekkebb, was founded in Kristiansand in 1875.

Below: Christiansholm fortress
Bottom: Kardemomme By Wildlife Park

trade and shipbuilding that brought new impetus, but more recently it has been the improved road, rail and waterways infrastructure, and the town's position as the administrative capital of southern Norway that have pushed its population up to around 75,000, and made it the fifth-largest town in the country.

Nowhere else in Norway better displays Christian IV's passion for building than Kristiansand. Occupying a strategic position at the southern tip of Norway and at the mouth of the Otra, the town was designed with a chequerboard layout by the Danish king. Despite several fires, the rectangular pattern was always retained.

The many traditional, white board houses in part of the old town are characteristic of the south coast cities. The city also plays host to the Quart Festival and the International Church Music Festival.

POSEBYEN

Of particular interest is the oldest district of ★ **Posebyen**. between Gyldenløvesgate and Kristian IV gate; with many traditional houses, this is the largest area of timber structures in the whole of Europe. Look out for ★ **Det Gamle Hospital ❶** in the Tordenskjoldgate (1709), and an 18th-century patrician house on the corner of Gyldenløvesgate and Vestre Strandgate.

The lawns around the ★★ **Christiansholm fortress ❷** (1672) attract sun-starved inhabitants as early as May. Also of note is the Gothic-Revival **Cathedral** (Domkirke), built in 1885 and the third largest church in Norway. It is one of many concert venues in the town, which is famous for its sacred, classical and rock music concerts and festivals.

Some 11km (7 miles) east of the city centre by the E18 lies the **Kristiansand Zoo** (open daily 10am–6pm). Here you can see a recreated Scandinavian wilderness with wolves, lynxes and other animals. All Norwegian children are familiar with ★★ **Kardemomme By ❸** or Cardamom Town', which was the subject of a popular story by Thorbjørn Egner entitled The Robbers of Kardemomme. Kardemomme By comprises a life-size version of his town. In addition Kristiansand Zoo has a forested park, an entertainment park and a water park (only open summer) with slides.

GIMLE GÅRD

The ★ **Gimle Gård** (tel: 38 10 26 80), 2km (1¼ miles) east of the town centre in Gimlemoen, is a splendid manor house dating from the early 19th century. Now a museum, it houses a collection of paintings, period furniture and porcelain. It was built by a shipping tycoon, Bernt Hol, and passed down the family (with a five-year interruption during the war) until it was bequeathed to the town and opened to the public in 1985. The **Setesdalbanen** (Railway Museum) is just north of the city and has a narrow-guage railway.

Norway's southernmost point may not be as popular a destination as the North Cape, but it offers a fine view out over the skerries and the open sea. When the sea is rough many people head for ★ **Lindesnes** to enjoy the spectacle. If the weather is fine and it is still light, the public are allowed to climb to the top of the lighthouse, where there is also a small musem.

The islands about 5km (3 miles) offshore are often mentioned in ancient Norse sagas as shelter for Viking ships sailing between Skagerrak and the North Sea.

Star Attractions
- Christiansholm fortress
- Kardemomme By

Below: catch of the day
Bottom: Lindesnes lighthouse

Map
below

High tea

For a bird's eye view of Trondheim, visit the 124-metre (407-ft) Tyholttårnet tele-communications tower. There is a revolving restaurant, Egon, on the way up (tel: 73 87 35 00).

4: Trondheim

In 1681 Trondheim suffered what practically every Norwegian town has suffered at some time – a serious fire, this being a hazard of using wood as the main building material. A new town was built. Military engineer Jean Caspar de Cicignon from Luxembourg centred his design on the peninsula at the mouth of the Nidelva river, and the present-day view from the market square along the two main streets, Munkegata and Kongensgate, gives a clear idea of the his intentions: wide roads in order to reduce damage from further fires. This and the colourfully painted wooden buildings lend the university city of Trondheim a special charm.

HISTORY

In the mid-11th century Trondheim (known then as Nidaros, meaning 'mouth of the River Nid'), now Norway's third-largest town with around 155,000 inhabitants, had a population of 1,000. At that time everything revolved around St Olav (Olav Haraldsson, who died in the Battle of Stik-

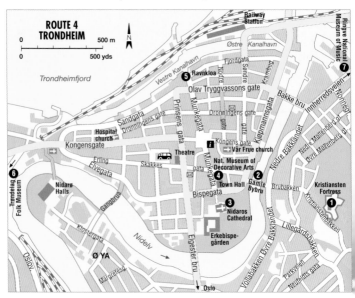

ROUTE 4
TRONDHEIM

lestad in 1030 and was buried here) and, until well into the 13th century, Trondheim was the seat of the Norwegian kings. By the time the country's first archbishopric was founded, in 1152, the town had become a shrine to St Olav, drawing pilgrims from near and far. Trondheim's position as a Scandinavian spiritual centre continued until the Reformation reached Norway in 1535. The fire of 1681 was also a serious blow to the town's prosperity, but the decline was soon reversed. In 1767, the country's first newspaper was published here; in 1814, Norway's first theatre opened its doors here. In 1877, when the railway line from Christiania (Oslo) was completed, Trondheim had already regained its status as a spiritual and commercial centre, surrounded by productive farmland.

Trondheim has always benefited from its position by the North Atlantic and its central location. Transport and trade, as well as technological research, still play an important part in its prosperity.

SIGHTS

The magnificent view down from the popular sunbathing spot by the ★ **Kristiansten fortress** ❶, or a walk through the picturesque **Nordre gate**, confirm the impression of Trondheim as a city that was carefully planned.

One of the most delightful areas of the city is around the ★★ **Gamle Bybru** ❷, the old drawbridge over the Nidelva river. Colourful old warehouses, some built on wooden stilts, line the banks, while to the east the **Bakklandet**, formerly the workers' quarter, rises steeply. This is a great place to stop for a drink or lunch.

THE CATHEDRAL

Following long-standing tradition, Norwegian kings are still crowned in the ★★★ **Nidarosdomen** or **Nidaros Cathedral** ❸, (Kongsgårds gate 2, tel: 73 53 91 60) considered one of the finest Gothic structures in Europe. Begun in 1070 and completed in stages, it displays late Romanesque and Gothic styles. Having suffered several fires,

Below: Trondheim waterfront
Bottom: Gamle Bybru

Map
on page
38

Stiklestad
On July 29, pilgrims gather at Stiklestad, north of Trondheim, to commemorate the death of King Olav Haraldsson, who died in battle here in 1030. St Olav, as he became, saw the formation of Norwegian unity and the adoption of the Christian faith. An open-air theatre production, with a cast of more than 300, re-enacts events of the time.

Fish market clock, Ravnkloa

restoration to the cathedral began in 1869, and was completed 132 years later in 2001.

If you're a fan of design and decor, head down Munkegata towards the ★ **National Museum of Decorative Arts** ❹ (Munkegata 3–7, tel: 73 80 89 50, open summer daily 10am–5pm, winter Tues–Sat 10am–3pm, Thur until 5pm, Sun noon–5pm). This is the stylish home of historical and modern collections of furniture, textiles, glass and silver. The Art Nouveau collection is especially strong and includes a room by the Belgian architect Henri Van de Velde, with Tiffany windows.

Continue down Munkegata and you'll arrive at ★ **Ravnkloa** ❺, the town's fish market. From here you can take a boat to the small island of ★ **Munkholmen** (Monk's Island), 2km (1¼ miles) offshore. Around the year 1000, it was a Benedictine monastery, and later a prison, with its most famous inmate being the Danish Count Peder Griffenfeld, who was imprisoned for 18 years.

MUSICAL MUSEUM

A good place to take a break is the ★ **Trøndelag Folk Museum** ❻ (Vertshuset, Sverresborg ålle, tel: 73 89 01 00), which has a pleasant restaurant called the **Tavern**, dating from 1739 and serving traditional Norwegian fare. Set around a 12th century fortification, there are open-air and indoor exhibitions, including a multimedia exhibition on Trøndelag's exciting past, called 'Images of Life'.

About 4km (2½ miles) north of the centre of Ringve is the ★ **Ringve National Museum of Music** ❼ (in Lade, overlooking the fjord, tel: 73 87 02 80), a fabulous museum for music lovers, with a large collection of musical instruments from all over the world. The Museum in the Barn, opened in 1999, illustrates the development of music through the ages. In the summer, musicians wear traditional costumes and play old instruments. If time is limited, a walk in the Botanical Gardens, a delightful setting for the museum, is very enjoyable.

5: Tromsø

In Tromsø (pop. 62,000), home to the northernmost university in the world, the sun shines more on average than in Mallorca, the bright nights are always lively, fish are landed in just the same way as they were centuries ago, and people who visit the place usually want to come back. There is an international film festival and the Northern Lights Music Festival during the cold, dark January nights, and in summer you can look forward to Mack's beer and seagulls' eggs, coastal culture and Midsummer Night festivals. The Tromsøers certainly know how to enjoy themselves – there are more bars per person here than anywhere else in Norway. The town has even been described as 'the Paris of the North'.

Map below

Tromsøsund

HISTORY
The town was established around 1250, and although Tromsø only received its municipal char-

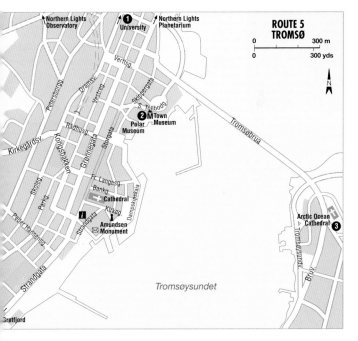

ROUTE 5 TROMSØ

Northern Lights Observatory

❶ University

Northern Lights Planetarium

Vertsg.

Petersborg

Dramsv.

Vestreg.

Skippergata

S. Tollbg.

Rådhusg.

❷ M Town Museum

Polar Museum

Kirkegårdsv.

Kongsbakken

Grønnegata

Storgata

Kirkeg.

Skolegt.

Fr. Langesg.

Banka

Cathedral

Kirkeg.

Dampskipskaia

Parkg.

ℹ

Strandgata

Amundsen ✉ Monument

Peter Hansensg.

Tromsøbrua

Arctic Ocean ▷ Cathedral ❸

Tromsøysundv.

Bruv.

Tromsøysundet

Strandgata

Grøtfjord

Below: Tromsø's cable car
Bottom: the Polar Museum

ter in 1794, this had more to do with objections from its competitors, Trondheim and Bergen.

By the end of the 19th century, Tromsø had become a major Arctic trade centre, and many of the Arctic expeditions originated here, giving rise to its second nickname: 'Gateway to the Arctic'. Now British, Dutch, German and Russian ships converge on Tromsø. Fishing is of prime importance, and today the town boasts four large filleting factories as well as the country's largest shrimp-processing plant and three herring factories.

In terms of surface area, Tromsø is Norway's largest town, but commerce and cultural life are concentrated on the small island of Tromsøy in the Tromsøsund. For a great view of the town and the sound, you can take the cable car *(fjellheisen)* up the Storsteinen, Tromsø's local mountain, 422m (1,385ft) above sea level.

THE UNIVERSITY

The interesting design of the ★ **University ❶**, a functional complex in the Breivika district, has attracted considerable acclaim, with the campus's 'Labyrinth' a fascinating focal point. In the nearby **Northern Lights Planetarium** you can admire a projection of the *aurora borealis* all year. It may be small but the ★★ **Polar Museum ❷** (open all year, hours vary; tel: 77 68 43 73) is very infor-

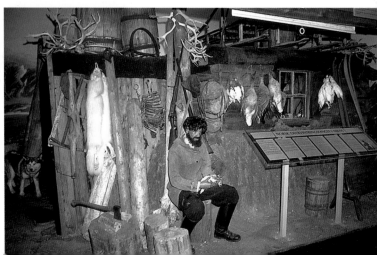

mative. One exhibition is devoted to the explorer, Roald Amundsen (1872–1928), who set out from Tromsø on his last expedition. Another centre dedicated to the polar world is ★★ **Polaria**, complete with IMAX cinema, a tunnelled aquarium, and exhibitions on arctic research (open daily summer 10am–7pm, winter noon–5pm; tel: 77 75 01 00). The centre is recognisable by its unusual design, which resembles toppling blocks of ice.

ARCTIC OCEAN CATHEDRAL

But the most important sight is Tromsdal Church or ★★ **Arctic Ocean Cathedral** ❸, as it is more commonly known, over on the mainland (open June–mid-Aug Mon–Fri 9am–7pm, Sun 1–7pm, mid-Aug–May daily 4–6pm). It is a magnificent structure, whose shape and colours symbolise the dark months of the year and the Northern Lights. Europe's largest stained-glass window – depicting the second coming – fills the east wall.

EXCURSIONS

If you do not have your own transport, ask at the tourist office at Storgata 61 for information about bus trips into the surrounding area. A round trip combining bus and boat is highly recommended for the dramatic scenery. The bus takes you northwards out to the Lyngen Peninsula, with a superb view of the Lyngen mountains (*see page 96*).

GRØTFJORD

There are a number of possiblities for visitors with their own transport. Heading west from Tromsø to the little village of **Tromvik** (50km/31 miles), for example, is a return to nature. Very narrow in parts, the road passes over the mountains and leads down the fjord to ★★ **Grøtfjord**, a village hidden like a pearl in the landscape. Locals claim that the sandy beaches here are the prettiest in northern Norway. Certainly, the view of the sea at the end of the arduous trek is the high spot of this delightful excursion.

Star Attractions
● Polar Museum and Polaria
● Arctic Ocean Cathedral
● Grøtfjord

Coldest beers
Mack brewery, Europe's northernmost and established in 1845, is a short walk from the centre of Tromsø. It has a beer hall and is famous for its Arctic Ale.

The Arctic Ocean Cathedral represents the shape of a Sami tent and the iciness of a glacier.

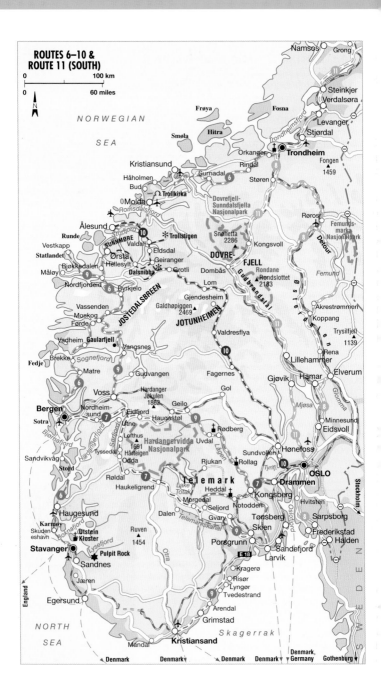

ROUTES 6–10 & ROUTE 11 (SOUTH)

0 — 100 km

0 — 60 miles

N

NORWEGIAN SEA

Namsos Grong

Steinkjer Verdalsøra

Frøya Fosna

Levanger

Smøla Hitra Stjørdal

Orkanger Trondheim

Kristiansund Rindal Fongen 1459

Håholmen Surnadal Støren

Bud Trollkirka

Molde Dovrefjell-Sunndalsfjella Nasjonalpark Røros

Femunds-marka Nasjonalpark

Ålesund Trollstigen Snøhetta 2286 Kongsvoll

Runde SUNNMØRE Valdal DOVRE-FJELL

Vestkapp Ørsta Eldsdal

Statlandet Hellesylt Geiranger Dombås Rondane Rondslottet 2183 Femund

Måløy Bjørkedalen Dalsnibba Grotli

Nordfjordeid Byrkjelo Lom Gjendesheim Akrestrømmen

Vassenden Galdhøpiggen 2469 Koppang

Moskog JOTUNHEIMEN Trysilfjell 1139

Førde Valdresflya Rena

Vadheim Gaularfjell Vangsnes Lillehammer

Fedje Brekke Sognefjord Elverum

Matre Gudvangen Fagernes Gjøvik Hamar

Voss Hardanger Jøkulen 1862 Gol Minnesund

Bergen Nordheim-sund Geilo Eidsvoll

Sotra Eidfjord Haugastøl Rødberg Sundvollen

Lofthus 1691 Utne Uvdal Hønefoss

Sandvikvåg Hardangervidda Nasjonalpark Rjukan Rollag OSLO

Stord Tyssedal Odda Drammen

Røldal Telemark Kongsberg

Haukeligrend Heddal Notodden Hvitsten

Haugesund Morgedal Seljord Tønsberg Sarpsborg

Karmøy Dalen Gvary Skien Frederikstad

Skudeneshavn Utstein Kloster Ruven 1454 Porsgrunn Sandefjord Halden

Stavanger Pulpit Rock Larvik

Sandnes Jæren Kragerø Risør Lyngør Tvedestrand

Egersund Arendal Grimstad

NORTH SEA Kristiansand Skagerrak

Mandal

Denmark Denmark Denmark Denmark Denmark, Germany Gothenburg

England Sognefjord Bjørnafjord Hardangerfjord Boknafjord Lysefjord Østerdal Gudbrandsdal Mjøsa Glomma Oslofjord Trondheimsfjord Romsdalsfjord JOSTEDALSBREEN Telemarkskanal SWEDEN Stockholm

Map opposite

6: The land of fjords and ferries

Stavanger – Bergen – Molde – Trondheim (869km/540 miles)

The E39 is the main west-coast artery. The North Sea is never very far away and, with countless fjords to cross, you are bound to make fairly slow progress. Tolls for ferries, tunnels and bridges also add to the cost of travel.

Fjord Norway, as this part of the country likes to call itself, offers an almost unimaginable range of landscapes – the open sea, fjords, skerries, islands and places that have grown up over the centuries in sheltered spots. And then there are those villages where the daily newspaper does not arrive until the afternoon and where the inhabitants much prefer to keep their thoughts to themselves. Fjord Norway is about walking on sandy beaches, over cliffs, through woods and way up into the mountains. The view from the water in this part of the country is a rare pleasure.

If you are travelling by bus, then you ought occasionally to make a detour down to the sea. Rather pricey catamaran ferries serve the smaller villages and islands.

Red herrings
Stavanger became famous for canning in the late 19th century when brisling (small herring) were cured and canned and sent as Norwegian 'sardines' all over the world.

Below: canned fish from (bottom) Stavanger

STAVANGER

When exploitation of 'black gold' commenced in the North Sea in the late 1960s, **Stavanger** (pop. 112,000) became Norway's oil capital and the town grew prosperous: in the fjord off Rogaland's administrative centre, rigs and orange supply ships bear witness to the new riches.

If you take a walk through the city's streets, then you will get the impression of a prosperous, if rather chaotic place. Only the central area between the harbour and the lake has any real appeal. Here, the old timber houses have been renovated and the original Stavanger, with cobbles and traffic-free shopping streets, has been revived. The 12th-century ★ **cathedral** (Domkirke), which dominates the most attractive part of the city, also protects this old quarter from traffic routes.

Map on page 44

JÆREN

There are numerous possibilities for excursions from Stavanger. Norway's most attractive sandy beaches are found in the **Jæren** region to the south of the town. If the weather is fine, then a tour along Highway 44 as far as Egersund and then back along the E39 (166km/ 103 miles) makes a perfect day trip. If you want to go for a swim, sunbathe in the dunes or observe the sea birds, then take a detour along Highway 507 and follow the North Sea coast. There are actually very few places in western Norway that look out over open sea.

Below: Jæren's sandy coast
Bottom: Pulpit Rock

GATEWAY TO THE FJORDS

Two of Norway's best-known picture-postcard images are sufficient to give Stavanger the title 'Gateway to the Fjords'. Start by taking the ferry across to Tau and then follow Highway 13 to the southeast for 15km (9 miles) to Botne, before following a mountain road for about 6km (4 miles).

A stiff two-hour walk or horse ride through heather moor and scrubland will then bring you to the flat top of the highly impressive ★★★ **Pulpit Rock** (Prekestolen), which drops vertically a dizzying 600m (2,000ft) into the ★★ **Lysefjord**. The tremendous view will only steady your nerves if you have a good head for heights. Look directly below and you will see the pleasure boats on the

fjord. Lysefjord cruises leave Stavanger every day and these provide a more comfortable way of viewing the rock. As well as showing visitors this amazing natural spectacle, the cruises also offer an insight into the history of Norwegian water power. For further information about fjord cruises, enquire at the tourist office in Stavanger (see page 119).

BYFJORD TUNNEL

A few kilometres north of Stavanger, the road disappears into the 5,860-m (6,410-yd) Byfjord tunnel. Opened in 1992, it is the longest underwater tunnel in Scandinavia (a hefty toll fee is payable when you finally emerge).

After a bridge, you descend into another tunnel, this time for 4,405m (4,817yds). Travellers would be hard pressed to appreciate the skerry landscape, were it not for the junction between the two tunnels that leads to the island of Mosterøy and the 12th-century ★★ **Utstein Kloster**. This historic monastery makes a beautiful setting for concerts, and the coastal area close to the monastery garden is a feast for the eyes. For more information about trips to the monastery, enquire at the tourist office in Stavanger.

KARMØY

Western Norway will continue to be dependent on car ferries for a long time to come, as tunnels and bridges across the wider fjords are too expensive to build, even in Norway. There are a number of ferry services operating between the islands and peninsulas of the west coast. This route north from Stavanger begins with a ferry across the Boknafjord to **Karmøy**, the island at the south of the outer islands chain. The ferry arrives at the port of **Skudeneshavn**, with its picturesque white, wooden houses and narrow streets.

Karmøy's history dates back to saga times when it was the 'North-way' that gave Norway its name. It's worth exploring the burial mounds near the east-coast town of **Korpervik** and, further north, the town of **Avaldsnes** with St Olav's Church.

★

Star Attractions
● Pulpit Rock
● Lysefjord
● Utstein Kloster

Liberty's origin
Copper used to cover the Statue of Liberty in New York came from one of the Visnes mines on the island of Karmøy.

Skudeneshavn

Map
on page
44

The north of the island is linked to the main-land again just south of **Haugesund**, the first size-able coastal town north of Stavanger. Haugesund has become prosperous through oil, and it is an important festival and congress centre. Numer-ous fjords and lakes cut into the surrounding peninsula, making it ideal for fishing, rowing, sailing, canoeing, diving and walking.

*Below: Skudeneshavn
seahouses
Bottom: Sognefjord*

STORD

The ferry from **Skjærsholmane** (104km/65 miles) carries travellers over to the southern tip of the island of ★ **Stord**. Stord and its two big neighbours **Bømlo** and **Tynesøy** form part of the southwest district of **Sunnhordland**. According to the sagas, it was on these islands that St Olav first introduced Christianity to Norway in 1024.

An upland ridge on Stord reaches nearly 750m (2,460ft) and the view stretches east to the Har-dangerfjord and the white sheet of the Folgefonn Glacier, and south towards Haugesund. There are sails everywhere, as well as the trails of express boats and various pleasure craft, and it makes a good paddling-off point for sea canoe-ing, from island to island, or into the mouth of the Hardanger.

The ferry for the Bergen peninsula leaves from Sandvikvåg at the northern end of Stord. A sec-ond island district, **Nordhordaland**, begins north of **Bergen** *(see page 30)*.

Near **Steinestø** (188km/117 miles), an impres-sive pontoon bridge carries traffic across the fjord. On the other side lies a landscape which can only be fully appreciated when the sun shines. If the grey clouds over the Nordhordaland region and the **Romarheim valley** are slowly pushing westward, it becomes apparent just how barren western Nor-way would be without its fjords and the sea. You are likely to see more sheep than people, golden eagles circle above, and the few villages seem asleep even on bright, sunny days.

Visit the **Barony Rosendal** (1661; May–Sept 11am–3pm daily), said to be the smallest castle in Scandinavia and now a museum.

BREKKE

Further north beyond Matre, engineers have blasted three long tunnels out of the mountain, thereby shortening the journey to the Sognefjord. You reach the Sognefjord at ★ **Brekke** (280km/ 174 miles), a beautiful village that has become quieter since the E39 and a busy ferry terminal moved to Oppedal.

With its huge beech tree, the Lovisendal mansion (1750) – for many years the seat of the provincial judge – dominates the village. At this point, the 200-km (125-mile) ★★★ **Sognefjord**, the longest fjord in the world, opens out in full splendour.

FEDJE

Near the mouth of the Sognefjord is the lovely island of ★★ **Fedje** (pop. 700), a popular target for sailing picnics and holidays. The ferry journey takes 30 minutes from Sævrøy docks. The two working lighthouses on the island bear witness to its continuing importance as a navigation point. You can even stay overnight in the Hellisøy lighthouse for a reasonable price, which includes use of the local power boat (tel: 56 16 43 20). Huge oil tankers glide through the channel to the north on their way to and from the huge Mongstad refinery. Gone are the days when all the men went whaling or fishing for shoals of herring off Fedje. The island's two whaleboats sail north in the sum-

Star Attractions
● Sognefjord
● Fedje

Below: traditional costume
Bottom: Fedje

Map on page 44

mer to catch the permitted quota of 30 or so Minke whales, the sardine factory is now a pewter factory and the salmon smokehouse is on another island.

FJORDS AND GLACIERS

On the northern side of the Sognefjord lies the region known as **Sogn og Fjordane**, which is not only famous for its deep fjords, its jagged coastline, mountains and glaciers, but also for its puritanism, temperance and, last but not least, for its American 'country' culture. Large cars belonging to Country and Western musicians who are invited here from the US are a common sight.

This area represents some 6 percent of Norway's surface area, but only 110,000 people live here out of a total population of around 4½ million. It may be something to do with all the pristine countryside, but the 'Sogninger' are far healthier and live even longer than other Norwegians. Agriculture, fishing and tourism provide most of the jobs, and places such as **Vadheim** (311km/193 miles) and **Førde** a little further north make interesting stopping-off points on the way to the 'Land of the Fjords and Glaciers'.

By the time you get to **Vassenden** (366km/227 miles), the rigours of the coastal climate have long been left behind. The town is situated at the western extremity of the ★★**Jølstervatn**, a huge lake

Below: glacier exploration
Bottom: a fjord ferry

below the foothills of the mighty 487 sq km (188 sq mile) ★★★**Jostedalsbreen** glacier, Europe's largest. The fine sand on its banks, verdant meadows and a mild wind are good enough reasons for a lengthier stop.

There are lakeside art galleries to visit and, if you have time to spare, you should take the southern shore to the ★★**Astruptunet** farmstead (open May–Sept, tel: 57 72 67 67). One of west Norway's most celebrated painters, Nikolai Astrup (1880–1928), lived here and many of the themes that occur in his paintings are reflected in the natural scenery surrounding the lake.

VÅTEDAL

Near **Byrkjelo** (409km/254 miles) you will arrive in the **Våtedal** valley, famous for its goats – many enjoy persuading tourists to part with some of their picnic. The **Nordfjord** region depends on cattle and breeding Norwegian ponies. Riding holidays with these tough creatures have been popular for many years. North of the small town of Nordfjordeid is ★**Bjørkedal**, celebrated for the traditional boat-building skills of its local residents. Every year in August a regatta is held on the lake here.

Volda (483km/300 miles) is an important high-school centre for the **Sunnmøre** region. The main road runs via Ørsta between the fjord and the ★★**Sunnmøre Alps**. Plunging straight into the sea, these mountains were one of the early targets for the many British climbers who first made Norway's mountains known. The road continues to the Festøy-Solevåg ferry, and, just beyond, branches off to **Ålesund** *(see page 80)*.

RUNDE

Some 10 percent of the population of the county of **Møre and Romsdal** lives on islands, and for most of the island communities fish is the mainstay of their livelihood. Anglers and divers pursue them, and thousands of sea birds, too, depend on them – reason enough for a detour to visit the island of ★**Runde** in the far west of Sunnmøre.

Star Attractions
● Jølstervatn
● Jostedalsbreen glacier
● Astruptunet
● Sunnmøre Alps

A short walk
In 1957 one of Norway's shortest laws was passed, enshrining the rights of skiers and walkers. It simply stated: 'At any time of the year outlying property may be crossed on foot, with consideration and due caution'.

Birdwatching in Runde

Map on page 44

The bird colony is situated on the 300-m (1,000-ft) cliffs known as the **Rundebranden**, and attracts professional and amateur naturalists from all over the world. Kittiwakes and puffins form the bulk of the colony, but altogether some 32 different sea birds nest here. They line the cliffs in their hundreds of thousands, and when they fly, it looks like a gigantic swarm of insects has darkened the sky. Two-hour birdwatching boat trips are available from the harbour.

Over the centuries, many heavily laden ships have run aground off the island. The most famous treasure was discovered in 1972 in the wreckage of the Dutch ship *Akerendam*, which sank here in 1725.

MOLDE

At **Spjelkavik** the route bends eastwards towards **Molde** (600km/372 miles). With no fewer than 87 snowcapped peaks within view, the ferry crossing to the 'City of Roses' is an unforgettable journey. Molde can look back on a long history as a fishing town. Displays of fishing equipment and boats in the ★ **Fishing Museum** on the island of **Hjertøya** recreate the everyday life of the coastal dwellers. Its other highlights are its football team and acclaimed international jazz festival, which takes place for one week a year in mid-July.

The **Nordmøre** region between the fjords in the south and the rugged coast is very popular with walkers. About 30km (19 miles) northwest of Molde is the ★★ **Troll Church**, a fantastic spectacle carved out of rock by the elements. This cave is situated about an hour and a half's walk from the road and is almost 380m (1,240ft) above sea level. Consisting of three chambers, it is about 70m (230ft) long.

THE ATLANTIC ROAD

In recent years the route from Molde to Kristiansund has become something of an attraction in itself. The ★ **Atlantic Road** (toll payable) consists of 12 bridges and stone embankments, which link

the islands and holms. If the wind is strong, motorists may have the impression that they are actually driving through the sea.

In 1968 the last fishermen left the village of ★ **Håholmen** on the Atlantic Road. Revived by Ragnar Thorseth, who sailed around the world, and Thorseth's wife, the village is now a quirky holiday resort with a restaurant and a bed-and-breakfast establishment.

Star Attraction
● **Troll Church**

KRISTIANSUND

Kristiansund (pop. 18,000; 682km/424 miles) is the last town on this journey through the fjords of Norway. Harbour boats link the town's islands, at one of which, **Vågen**, is the Coastal Culture Centre which preserves traditional shipbuilding skills. You can gain a good impression of Kristiansund from the **Varden** viewpoint near the town centre – where you also bid farewell to the coast.

There is one more ferry crossing before the road winds its way past narrow fjords as far as **Skei** (745km/463 miles), struggles up past the winter sports resort of **Rindal** and then accompanies the Orkla river through wooded valleys to the fjord in **Orkanger** (825km/ 513 miles). The waters of the Surna and the Orkla are popular among salmon fishermen. From here it is only 44km (27 miles) to **Trondheim** (*see page 38*).

Below: coastal culture
Bottom: Molde panorama

Map
on page
44

Biodiversity
Hardangervidda is Europe's largest mountain plateau, covering 10,000 sq km (3,860 sq miles). Around 120 species of bird breed on these upland moors, and there are more than 400 plant species, due to the plateau's two distinct climates in the gentle west and the harsher east.

7: From east to west

Oslo – Kongsberg – Telemark – Rjukan – Hardangerfjord – Bergen (525km/326 miles)

This route takes you from one side of the country to the other. You'll head from the east with its densely populated conurbations, through the wooded Telemark area with its delightful villages and rural traditions, on past the barren *vidda* and the Hardangerfjord, the orchard of Norway.

You'll then go on to the west, to the open sea and bare rocks where rare birds, divers and anglers have found their little piece of paradise. Visitors will be impressed by the countless tunnels that make up the Haukeli Pass – they form a vital part of what is one of the few winter links between east and west.

KONGSBERG

Kongsberg (pop. 23,000; 80km/50 miles), Norway's first industrial town, came to prominence after silver was discovered there. The town takes its name, King's Mountain, from the interest shown in the mines by Christian IV, who visited them many times.

Today the old silver mine can be viewed only by prior arrangement (tel: 32 72 32 00). But you can head for the mines in ★ **Saggrenda**, 7km (4 miles) from the town centre. A narrow-gauge train carries visitors 2.3km (1½ miles) into the mountain to a point 342m (1,122ft) beneath the surface. Silver was first discovered here in 1623 and, with the assistance of German engineers, mining operations once kept 4,000 men in work. When the mine was abandoned in 1957, it was calculated that some 1,300 tons of the precious metal had been dug out in the course of 334 years. The ★★ **Norwegian Mining Museum** housed in the smelting plant (1842) documents the early days of silver mining in Kongsberg, the development of mining techniques and, not least, the day-to-day toil which went on below ground. At the ★ **Royal Mint Museum** in the same building, there is an almost complete collection of Norwegian coins.

Saggrenda silver mine

INTO TELEMARK

The E134 westward leads into the heart of **Telemark**, beginning with the town of **Heddal** (118km/73 miles). The ★★ **stave church** here, which was built between 1147 and 1242, is the biggest and most impressive one of its kind in the country. Its best-known feature is a doorway which is richly carved with animal ornamentation and human faces. The people of Telemark remain masters at expressing nature through art, and nowhere is this more evident than in the wonderful rose paintings in the Ramberg room of the ★ **Heddal Bygdetun** farmhouses.

You will see the characteristic dark brown, moss-covered farmhouses and *stabbur*, or barns on stilts, everywhere. During the summer, there will always be dancing, but in the winter it is skiing that preoccupies the inhabitants. The history of Telemark, the region between the south coast and the mountains, between the sophisticated east and the fjords in the west, is recounted in numerous songs and poems.

Farmsteads by tranquil lakes between the verdant hillsides have grown into little villages. Silversmiths continue to make a living, while wood carving, rose painting, poetry, folk music and dancing are still as popular as ever. In Telemark, nature and the perspective of the people are reflected in primitive Norwegian art. Tourist Information, tel: 35 90 00 30.

Star Attractions
● Norwegian Mining Museum
● Heddal stave church

Below: Heddal stave church
Bottom: roadside meadow
en route to Bergen

Map on page 44

SELJORD

The Telemarkers like to show pride in their region; residents of **Seljord** (174km/108 miles) also love to boast about their 'monster'. The young, the old and even police officers, claim to have seen a giant sea-snake in the local lake. Given the marvellous scenery and the unusual light conditions during the summer, it is only too likely that the Loch Ness monster's sister should decide to make her home here. Why she is so shy, though, is hard to say. Perhaps it is because there are too many tourists, who now set out in boats on to the lake in the hope of catching a glimpse of the beast. At any rate, divers are advised not to get too close to Seljord's biggest attraction.

Further west you'll reach **Morgedal**. Sondre Nordheim lived here from 1825 to 1897; he is usually credited with making this little Telemark town the cradle of modern skiing, for it was he who invented bindings to give skiers control over their heels, enabling them to negotiate curves (the Telemark method). *'Slalåm!'* was born.

WARTIME RESISTANCE

The folklore of Telemark is not limited to age-old traditions and skiing, however. During World War II the region witnessed the most celebrated act of resistance in Norway, when, in February 1943, a team of saboteurs went in to blow up the Vemork

Below: a friendly face
Bottom: around Heddal

heavy water plant near **Rjukan**, an event re-enacted in the 1965 film *The Heroes of Telemark* with Kirk Douglas and Richard Harris.

The town can be reached by turning right off the highway at Ofte, along Highway 37, adding an extra day to your journey. No visitor to Rjukan, dwarfed and darkened by mountains all round, could fail to be awed by the audacity of the mission. More importantly, though, the production of heavy water in the plant was a race which, if it hadn't been stopped, could conceivably have given Hitler the atomic bomb. The struggle for control of the plant took over two years, involved four assaults and claimed 92 lives.

INDUSTRIAL WORKER'S MUSEUM

The Vemork heavy water plant is now partially an ★★ **Industrial Worker's Museum** (tel: 35 09 90 00). In addition to information here, the town library has a good collection of literature about the operation, including some books written by those who participated.

The story of the heroes of Telemark began with a joint British and Norwegian mission, which attempted to get men into the area by glider, but ended disastrously when one of the towing aircraft crashed. This was followed by the successful all-Norwegian affair, involving the parachuting of six men to join up with an advance party on the ground, the daring entry into the plant, the laying of charges and the escape just in the nick of time before the cataclysmic explosion. The heroics only came to an end after the saboteurs' 400-km (250-mile) journey on skis to safety in Sweden, with German soldiers in hot pursuit.

HYDRO-ELECTRICITY

In Norway, Rjukan is also synonymous with hydro-electric power, and the town's main street bears the name of Norsk Hydro's founder, Samuel Eyde. In the town of Dalen, buried about 300m (1,000ft) inside a mountain, is the enormous old **Mår Power Station** (open summer weekdays only, free tours,

Star Attraction
● **Industrial Worker's Museum**

Telemark skiing
There has been a recent revival in 'Telemark' skiing, a method which uses only one pole. It was developed in the 19th century by Sondre Norheim, who designed bindings and sidecuts to give control over skis. In 1868 he and local farmers skiied 180 km (112 miles) to Oslo where they inspired a craze for ski jumping.

Kirk Douglas in The Heroes of Telemark

Map
on page
44

Below: the Krossobanen
Bottom: Låtefossen waterfall

tel: 35 09 12 90). The longest wooden staircase in the world is beside the down pipes – 3,875 steps over a distance of 1,270m (1,390yds). When Norsk Hydro started work on the project in 1907, there were just a few farmsteads in the narrow valley between the Hardangervidda and the Gaustafjell, but by 1920 Rjukan had a population of 8,350, nearly all of whom depended on the power station and chemical factories for their livelihood.

Norsk Hydro continues to produce gas and electricity here to this day, but you do not have to spend hours climbing stairs to see the power of water. With the ★ **Krossobanen** cable car, it only takes five minutes to climb to **Gvepseborg**, 886m (2,907ft) above sea level. The view towards the Gaustatoppen mountain (1,883m/6,178ft) is superb. If you are fit, a hike to the summit is an option, but it will take three hours. Start out from the car park in **Stavsro** (13km/8 miles south of Dale).

LAKE TOTAK

Return to the main highway by the delightful route along the northern shore of **Lake Totak** via Rauland. **Haukeligrend** (264km/164 miles) has a motel with cafeteria, motor mechanic, bus stop and supermarket. This is also where Highway 9 from the Setesdalen valley joins this route, marking the boundary between Telemark and western Norway. It is uphill from now on, as trees become dwarf birches and hills give way to mountains.

Near **Røldal** (318km/197 miles) the route passes through almost 40km (25 miles) of tunnel. The twin waterfalls in ★ **Låtefossen** drop almost 180m (590ft) and set the tone for Hardangerfjord ahead.

ODDA

Odda (pop. 8,000; 361km/224 miles) lies at the southern end of the pretty **Sørfjord**, the southern arm of the Hardangerfjord. Despite its beautiful setting, a huge industrial complex lines the shores. For 80 years, the town's prosperity depended on the smelting factory where a variety of metals were processed. Its best years are now over, and the water, earth and air are slowly recovering. By the Sørfjord, north of Odda, set in a rather hostile environment beneath sombre, avalanche-prone precipices, is ★ **Tyssedal** (pop. 1,100), a village with an interesting industrial past.

In 1906, migrant workers built Norway's first electricity generating station here, using the vast quantities of water that cascaded down from the Hardangervidda. Using internationally raised capital, the electricity operated a smelting furnace for titanium ore: Tinfos Titan Et Iron. This factory marked the beginning of Norway's industrial revolution. Way above the town the Folgefonn glacier glistens in the sunlight, while down below the early shift returns home from work.

HARDANGERFJORD

★★ **Lofthus**, an attractive spot situated before the town of Kinsarvik on Highway 13, epitomises the ★★★ **Hardangerfjord**: a village by the banks of the fjord, a few small firms (mainly connected to the timber trade), steep slopes and one large fruit orchard full of trees laden with apples, pears, plums, but mainly cherries. The monks from the Lyse monastery near Bergen were the first to exploit the stable climate and set about cultivating the hillside soil. They also laid the ★★ **Monks' Ascent** which starts at Opedal farm

Star Attractions
● Lofthus
● Hardangerfjord
● Monks' Ascent

Below and bottom: changing seasons in Hardangerfjord

Map on page 44

Below: Utne
Bottom: the Kinsarvik ferry

and rises up to the western edge of the Hardangervidda. The two-hour climb of 950m (3,120ft) is rewarded by a fine view over the green shores of the Hardangerfjord.

Nearly half a million fruit trees line the fjordside, turning it pink and white in spring, as the blossom is reflected in the deep, still water. At this time of year, the waterfalls are in full spate, shooting water dramatically over the sides of the mountains.

The Hardangerfjord provided inspiration for the composer Edvard Grieg, who was a regular summer visitor to the village of **Ullensvang** just to the south of Lofthus. Together with his companion, the violin virtuoso Ole Bull *(see page 31)*, he travelled on foot and horse in the area, learning old melodies and dipping into centuries-old cultural traditions and customs. His holiday cabin, Komponisten, is in the garden of the Hotel Ullensvang, and the eight-stringed Hardanger fiddle has become the archetypical Norwegian instrument. Hardanger Tourist Information, tel: 56 55 38 70.

UTNE

Continue now to **Kinsarvik** and take the ferry across to **Utne** (406km/252 miles) on the west side of the Sørfjord. There are good reasons to ignore the first ferry across to the north side of the Hardangerfjord and to linger awhile in this idyl-

lic village. The ★ **Hardanger Folk Museum** (tel: 53 67 00 40) is worth visiting, while the ★ **Utne Hotel** dates from 1722 and is the oldest hotel in Norway still in operation.

Most passengers on the ferry to **Kvanndal** stay on deck with video cameras running or camera shutters clicking as the Hardangerfjord opens up in the west, and in the east a seemingly impenetrable wall of mountains creates an incredibly beautiful sight.

Nordheimsund (446km/277 miles) is the last stop by the Hardangerfjord before the climb starts again – past ★★ **Steindalsfossen**, a waterfall beneath which you can walk and admire from behind, while staying dry, through countless tunnels and along terrifying gorges as far as **Bergen** (*see page 30*; 525km/326 miles).

Star Attraction
● **Steindalsfossen**

Canoeing waters
The island of Sotra is a great place for sea canoeing. Its small islands and rocky outcrops are full of interest and provide safe shelter. If you try sea fishing, the minimum size for keeping sea salmon, trout or char is 25cm (9.8in).

SOTRA

As a continuation of this route, you might want to consider visiting the 120-km (74-mile) long island of **Sotra**, which lies just off Bergen. Narrow sounds, hundreds of small islands and grey rock dominate the seaward side while, along the valleys in the island's interior, forests of fir trees rustle in the wind and meadowland flourishes. Sotra is a haven for divers, anglers and mountaineers of varying abilities.

TELAVÅG

In the north, in **Kollnes**, stands a giant gas terminal, where the raw material is stored before being forwarded to Germany and Belgium for consumption. In the south of the island are **Telavåg** and **Glesvær**. During the 'Night of Telavåg' in 1942, the Gestapo burnt the whole village to the ground in an act of vengeance, and all the men were deported to Germany.

A small museum and a memorial stone remain as reminders of this terrible event. The tiny fishing village of Glesvær is a miniature version of Sotra – an ancient trading port amid a delightful skerry landscape. *Havstrilen*, a two-mast sailing boat, regularly takes visitors out on trips into the North Sea.

Angling country

Map on page 44

Old road
For only 30 kroner, *Rock Carving Tour*, from tourist boards, is a useful guide to the history of the road between Fredrikstad and Sarpsborg.

8: Flat land and broad valleys

Fredrikstad – Oslo – Eidsvoll – Hamar – Røros – Trondheim (659km/409 miles)

Many people travel the 120km (74 miles) from Halden on the Swedish border to Oslo non-stop in 90 minutes – and miss out on the delightful countryside and the atypically Norwegian landscape, an area of industrial towns but also a granary, inhabited since the Bronze Age. Elks and wolves, forests of birch and fir trees, and meadows and villages bordering rivers and lakes – these all make up the Østerdalen region around the Glomma river from Elverum to Røros. Icy cold in winter, stable in summer, the climate here is typical of inland regions.

East Norwegians enjoy a largely rural life, many of them participating in outdoor pursuits such as hunting and sport fishing. Everything is quieter than in the west, but the traffic is denser. And yet the motor car is often not required. Cycling is a pleasant option and there are numerous opportunities for walking and canoeing.

FREDRIKSTAD

Some 30km (19 miles) from the Swedish border lies Norway's oldest fortified city and the industrial town of **Fredrikstad** (pop. 70,000), where the Glomma flows into the Oslofjord. The large port and proximity to Sweden and the European mainland are the main advantages of the location today. In the past, however, Swedish neighbours made life difficult for this region. After 1570 the Swedes set fire to Fredrikstad no fewer than 15 times, so in the 17th century the people built a wall around their town. By 1685, Fredrikstad, the strongest fortress in Norway, was completed. It was 1814 before the Swedes dared to attack again. After a few hours of siege, the myth of impregnability had been destroyed. Nowadays, the ★★ **fortress town** can be peacefully conquered on foot – at the same time, it is worth having a closer look at the ★ **Kongsten Fort** just south of the old town, and the childhood home of the South Pole traveller Roald Amundsen.

View from home

OLDTIDSVEIEN

Highway 110, an 18-km (11-mile) long stretch of road that runs between Fredrikstad and Sarpsborg, is known in Norway as the ★★ **Oldtidsveien** (Old-time way). To race along it in a car would be a pity. The meadows and woods to both left and right are dotted with ancient sites and monuments, with 3,000-year-old rock paintings (in **Begby**, **Hornnes** and **Solberg**) depicting farming and maritime themes, and burial mounds such as those at Hunn, most of which date from before AD 900.

In addition, there are Stone Age settlements and manor houses such as Nes farmstead where the main building dates from the 17th century. The 'Rock Carving Tour' gives archaeologists plenty of scope for excavation work, and is also a bridle path for walkers exploring these arable lands known as 'Norway's granary'.

EIDSVOLLBYGNING

Despite Oslofjord to the left and wooded walking country to the right, most motorists head straight along the E6 towards the capital. There are attractions along the way, however: **Lake Vannsjø** to the east of Moss is great for canoeing, and, at **Vestby** (77km/48 miles), the turn to **Hvitsten** leads to a white sandy beach and beautiful sunsets over the Oslofjord. As the suburbs of Oslo

Star Attractions
● **Fredrikstad fortress town**
● **Oldtidsveien**

Below: Viking heritage
Bottom: the coast near the Swedish border

Map on page 44

Below: Eidsvollbygning
Bottom: the Skibladner

expand, this region is becoming more popular. **Drøbak** is the nicest of these coastal towns.

It is actually well beyond Oslo, near Eidsvoll, that the countryside reappears. In **Råholt** and **Eidsvoll** (158km/98 miles) forestry management and saw mills are the main sources of employment. With 30,000 hectares (74,000 acres) of woodland, everything revolves around timber. What has put Eidsvoll on the map, however, is the ★★ **Eidsvollbygning**, the house of the factory owner Carsten Anker. Here, in May 1814, the Norwegian constitution was proclaimed by 112 men from all social classes. The building is now a museum and the site is a national monument.

BOAT TRIP

Eidsvoll is a port of call for the world's oldest paddle steamer, *Skibladner*. This vessel first sailed on **Lake Mjøsa** in 1856, and it still plies the villages from Eidsvoll to Hamar at about 25kmph (16mph), in summer. Norway's largest inland lake begins at the bridge at **Minnesund** (176km/109 miles). As the steamer glides past the meadows and wooded slopes, salmon and fresh strawberries are the traditional on-board fare. Large farmsteads border the eastern shore of the lake like pearls on a string. Clearly, cattle and forestry have provided their owners with a good living.

HAMAR

Hamar (pop. 28,000; 228km/141 miles) has also prospered from its lakeside location and the traffic between Oslo and Trondheim. Between 1569 and 1849 it was torched many times by the Swedes. After 1848 'New' Hamar grew rapidly. The three main sights in Hamar reflect the town's development. Before the Reformation, it was the seat of a bishop and the site of a monastery, and the ★ **cathedral ruins** at the lakeside are a legacy of this time. Recently, a spectacular glass cathedral was built around the existing ruins. Hamar was rejuvenated during the 19th century by the railway, and the ★ **Railway Museum**, established in 1896, is the oldest technical museum in Norway. Among the large collection is the early steam engine *Caroline*, built by Robert Stephenson in 1861. Fresh impetus was provided by the Winter Olympics of 1994, which centred on nearby Lillehammer. The main indoor ★ **skating arena** was built in Hamar; with a roof designed to look like the upturned hull of a Viking ship, it is an impressive structure and contains one of the fastest ice-skating rinks in the world.

Star Attraction
● **Eidsvollbygning**

Cheers!
For some good fiery local aquavit, visit the famous Løiten Brænderi distillery, which has been in business since 1855. Open in summer, it lies 18km (11 miles) east of Hamar towards Elverum (tel: 62 59 49 10).

THE SINGING WOODS

Lillehammer, at the far northern end of the lake, is covered in Route 11 *(see page 81)*. This route heads east from Hamar to **Elverum** (258km/160 miles) in the **Glomma** valley. Just beyond the town, the 'singing woods' begin, so take your walking shoes and mosquito net. The river flows north through the woods at great speed – everything else moves at a much gentler pace. At dusk during the late summer, elks emerge from the woods and approach the fruit orchards – one or two are bound to cross your path.

Rena (289km/180 miles), Koppang (347km/216 miles) and Tynset (449km/279 miles) are rather dull market towns. **Østerdalen** is all about disappearing into the countryside, with fishing tackle, guns for hunting, a canoe or just a tent; in the winter it is marvellous cross-country skiing terrain. For excellent downhill skiing, make for **Trysilfjellet** (70km/44 miles from Elverum on Highway 25).

Woodland orchid

Map on page 44

Royal rescue
Contestants in the Birke-beiner Race commemorate the trek that two warriors, Skjervald and Torstein, made in 1206 from Lillehammer to Østerdalen to save the 18-month-old prince Håkon Håkons-son from his enemies. Their legs were wrapped in birch bark (*birkebeiner* means 'birch legs') to protect them from the cold.

Skiing downhill

SKI RACING

Skiing is an obsession for many Norwegians, so there is nothing extraordinary about 7,000 cross-country skiers setting out on a 54-km (34-mile) course, climbing as high as 1,090m (3,576ft) above sea level and carrying a 3.5kg (8lb) weight in their rucksacks. The Birkebeiner race takes place in March near Rena and Lillehammer. A bicycle race and marathon are also held. Enquire at Lillehammer *(see page 81)* for further information.

The view of the forest to the east from Highway 3 beckons, so rather than continuing straight up the main road to Røros, a detour is recommended. In Koppang, leave the constant stream of caravans behind. From Åkrestrømmen the road branches off to the east, up through the dense forest. The occasional car parked by the roadside probably indicates an angler luring trout and whitefish to take the fly. Fish and game dominate everyday life in these parts.

ISTERFOSSEN FALLS

Take care at the **Isterfossen** waterfall at the southern end of ★ **Lake Femund**. The waters here are asking to be fished, but they are dangerous. Lake Femund is off the beaten track; this is 'Norway's Orient', as the poet Johan Falkberget once wrote, and cars are of little use here.

From **Femundsvika** or **Sorken** you will have to proceed on foot, in a canoe or by steamer. The lake and **Femundsmarka National Park** further east are unspoilt countryside and home to domesticated reindeer and musk ox. What makes the difference is the absence of dense undergrowth that might block the views of cold lakes, rivers full of fish and mountains pointing skyward. But be warned about the abundance of mosquitoes. They tend to home in on the ill-prepared, so make sure that you are carrying some insect repellent as well as a mosquito net.

RØROS

At ★★ **Røros** (pop. 5,500; 501km/311 miles) the two routes merge. An excursion to Lake Femund is feasible from here too, but first have a look round the town. Røros was the archetypal company town with life and society revolving around the mining of copper. Now the inhabitants earn their living from sawmills, making furniture, processing wool and reindeer meat, as well as tourism. Røros is a remote spot and the winters are harsh. The lowest temperatures in the whole of Norway are often recorded here and it is hard to keep the work going. However, the old town is on UNESCO's World Heritage List and at 628m (2,060ft) above sea level, Røros is the only 'mountain town' in Norway.

The wealthy folk lived to the east of the river in Bergmannsgate, while the workers had to make do with the east side beneath the slagheaps and the smelter. Røros' **Old Town** features 250-year-old workers' cottages, slagheaps, and engineers' houses, many owned by Germans who emigrated for the work.

Copper ore was first mined in Røros in 1644, but the last company went bankrupt in 1977. Picturesque log houses are all that remain. **Bergstadens Ziir**, a church dating from 1784, is the only stone structure in the town. Zirr means pearl in German, and the white church appears as a pearl among the brown cottages.

Follow Highway 30 to **Støren** (607km/377 miles). **Trondheim** (*see page 38*) is a further 52km (32 miles).

Star Attraction
● Røros

Below: Lake Femund
Bottom: Røros, Norway's
only 'mountain town'

Map
on page
44

9: From the South Cape to the West Cape

Kristiansand – Larvik – Geilo – Voss – Sognefjord – Vestkapp (935km/581 miles)

This coast-to-coast route starts in the Danish-style town of Kristiansand with its white, red-roofed wooden houses *(see page 35)*, heads north past bathing beaches and pretty ports, and then turns into the interior to the West Cape (Vestkapp), a rock that has been worn smooth by centuries of fierce storms.

Below: the Skagerrak coast at Grimstad
Bottom: cabin near Kragero

Along the route lie the forests of Telemark, mountains with skiing resorts and the Hardangervidda, the higher mountains north of the Sognefjord and the rugged west coast. Plenty of opportunities exist to test out your walking gear, but variations in landscape and climate do restrict activities. Between July and September, it is safe and restful, but before mid-May parts of this route are often choked with snow, making many of the higher elevations impassable.

THE RIVIERA OF THE NORTH

South of Oslo, the Skagerrak coast, facing south-east between Kristiansand and Larvik, is Norway's top destination for sun lovers. Thousands of holiday cabins *(hytter)* have been built on the

islands and holms, which is why the region is sometimes dubbed the 'Riviera of the North'.

Grimstad (pop. 19,000; 53km/33 miles), however, is a cultural centre. It was here where a young Henrik Ibsen lived for six years as an apprentice chemist, and where he wrote his first play, *Catilina*. The chemist's, which goes under the name of ★ **Ibsenhuset**, has been preserved in the style of 1837 and, together with the ★ **Town Museum**, is a magnet for Ibsen fans.

LYNGØR

Arendal prospered as a conduit for timber shipments abroad, including much of the timber used for the rebuilding of London after the 1666 Great Fire. In 1863 Arendal itself lost to fire the houses on stilts, which had earlier given it the name of Little Venice, but, overflowing onto a number of small islands, it retains its lovely setting.

The Arendal Bymuseum has extensive displays of local history and the **Rådhus** (Town Hall), built in 1815 in Empire style, is the tallest wooden structure in Norway.

★ **Tvedestrand** (pop. 6,000) is an attractive resort with a defensive outer harbour, which runs from island to island offshore. Settlement is uneven and extends up the hillsides into the woods. Among the houses, which at first sight look almost identical, are a number of surprises. The 'Smoothing Iron', for example, is said to be the narrowest house in Norway. Tourism and sailing are the town's mainstay.

Many visitors take the MS *Søgne* from here to ★★ **Lyngør**, the 'Venice by the Skagerrak'. This village surrounded by water is an idyllic spot with white-painted houses, colourful window boxes and no cars.

RISØR

★ **Risør**, the 'white town by the Skagerrak', is famous for its wooden boat festival, its art galleries and, not least, its attractive patrician houses. Situated at the end of a peninsula and pointing out

Star Attraction
● Lyngør

Small town Norway
Norway's great playwright Henrik Ibsen was born at Skien and grew up at Grimstad an unhappy young man. His experiences here contributed to his writing, and the searing exposure of goings on in small Norwegian towns, which caused such a scandal when the plays were first performed.

Ibsenhuset

Map
on page
44

Canal trips

The Vrangfoss waterfall is just one attraction of the Telemarkskanal. The waterway is served by pleasure boats and the Norwegian State Railway, which offers inclusive tickets from Oslo, while the tourist office in Skien (tel: 35 90 55 20) runs a variety of tours with bus connections. The local authority, Statens Vegvesen Telemark in Stein, can provide information (tel: 81 54 80 00).

Ibsen House, Skien

to the tiny offshore islands, its beaches attract Norwegians eager to make the most of the summer sun.

Porsgrunn and **Skien** (190km/118 miles) are heavily dependent on Norsk Hydro and other industries. Henrik Ibsen was born in Skien; **Ibsen House** is the town's cultural centre, with a large theatre, exhibition and concert halls. Ibsen's holiday home was in **Venstøp**, 5km (3 miles) from Skien, and today houses yet another Ibsen museum.

VRANGFOSS

Beyond lies the Telemark, and industry and urban sprawl are replaced by dense forests, Norwegian farming culture and a network of lakes and canals. Travellers can either explore the region by road (leave the E18 at Porsgrunn) or admire it from the water. Canals and rivers link the four large lakes between Skien in the southeast and **Dalen** at the western end of **Lake Bandak**. Manually operated locks negotiate the altitude difference of 72m (236ft). The 105-km (65-mile) long Telemark canal from Skien to Dalen was built between 1854 and 1892 and soon became a tourist attraction in its own right.

Some people stop off in **Ulefoss**, **Eidsfoss** or by the ★★ **Vrangfoss** to view the canal and locks from the bank, but most make the 10-hour cruise from Skien to Dalen and have their car transported to their destination.

UVDAL STAVE CHURCH

Back on the coast, Highway 40 begins in **Larvik** (197km/ 122 miles) and follows the **Numedal** and the **Lågen**, a salmon river, up into the mountains. It isn't until one reaches well beyond **Kongsberg** *(see page 54)*, near **Rødberg**, that the valley emerges from the clutches of the forest. Rødberg is only a tiny village with barely 500 inhabitants but, whenever power stations are hidden away inside hills, mountains are not far away.

Just a few kilometres beyond Rødberg, at **Uvdal**, is a superb example of a ★★ **stave church** (open daily June–mid-Aug 10am–6pm). Work on the church began at the end of the 12th century, but the sacristy at the north end was not added until 1819. Alterations in various architectural styles were made during the intervening years but it has retained its architectural harmony.

Vasstulan Mountain Centre, at an altitude of 1,100m (3,600ft), is the highest point on this tour. It offers fine views, a few log cabins and a guest-house, but hardly anyone stops off here for long. Most people continue to **Dagali** (420km/261 miles). This region is a paradise for hunters and anglers, although the open-air museum with traditional farm buildings (including a mill and stables) is also worth a visit, as is the Dagali Hotel, dating back to the 18th century. Cattle grazing has a long tradition in these parts, and the rich variety of fauna and flora is typical of an east Norwegian mountain valley.

Below: walking and (bottom) canoeing country

GEILO

Geilo (462km/287 miles), a busy tourist centre in summer, is Norway's most popular resort in winter. It can easily be identified from a distance as the wooded mountains nearby look as though they have been cut neatly with a razor blade. World slalom championships have been held here but the pistes are too short for downhill races. What-

Map
on page
44

Map
on page
44

Lemming squash
It is a myth that lemmings commit suicide. After a couple of years of low population density, a mild spring can result in a population explosion. Norwegian lemmings, which are around 15cm (6in) long, can have eight litters a year, with up to six young in each. This results in a mass migration from the mountains to the valleys during which many are eaten by predators and a great number die when they try to cross rivers and seas.

ever the season, it is worth taking the ★ **Geilo Taubane** chairlift to the top of the highest peak in the area. Many people then descend at their own pace along a choice of signposted trails.

Haugastøl (486km/302 miles) is the gateway to superb walking country, and there are nearly always groups of hikers waiting by the little station on the Oslo to Bergen railway. Some will be heading for **Finse**, the highest station on the line (1,222m/4,009ft above sea level), others will be setting out on foot across Europe's largest mountain plateau, the stunning ★★★ **Hardangervidda** *(see also page 54)*, The road cuts across the 10,000sq km (3,860 sq mile) bleak plateau for 70km (44 miles), but the landscape has a wealth of fauna and flora. You will probably encounter reindeer, arctic foxes and, during the regularly recurring 'lemming years' (when the rodents embark on a mass migration – *see panel on left)*, predatory birds – and ornithologists – abound.

HARDANGERJØKULEN

Although a network of footpaths spreads in all directions, no one should treat the *vidda* lightly. The watershed runs across the plateau and the weather can change suddenly. Wherever you are, the ★★ **Hardangerjøkulen** glacier on the northern edge sparkles in the sunlight. Even at the end

Local costumes, Voss

of June, snow can fall at the summit of the glacier, and so it is inadvisable to take long hikes across it before mid-July. For many walkers, the eternal ice of the glacier is the highlight of their tour, but it is always best to travel in groups and to pay attention to the weather forecast.

The ideal starting point for a trip into the heart of the *vidda* is the Halne Fjellstove hotel *(see page 123)*. The staff here provide an information service for walkers.

Star Attractions
- **Hardangervidda**
- **Hardangerjøkulen**
- **Vøringfossen**
- **Måbø Valley**

VØRINGFOSSEN

Vøringfossen

The ★★★ **Vøringfossen** is one of Norway's outstanding waterfalls. It has a perpendicular drop of 183m (600ft) down to the wild ★★ **Måbø Valley**, and there is a path at the top overlooking the fall which is not for those who suffer from vertigo. The waterfall is 'switched off' in the winter months to run turbines, but it is still possible to explore the valley from below. It is a tiring, but uniquely beautiful walk. Avalanche scree has accumulated in the gorge, yet the rich vegetation beneath the waterfall is compensation for your efforts. With a maximum of only two hours sun per day at the best of times, attractive ferns and flowers still manage to grow. Fjord Tours runs tours to the Hardanger Fjord and Vøringfossen waterfall (tel: 81 56 82 22).

Eidfjord (546km/339 miles) is a typical west Norwegian community: a village at the end of a fjord, a vast hinterland, enormous quantities of water – and high earnings from hydro-electric powerplants. Guided tours are organised around the ★ **Simadalen power station** during the summer.

The farm at nearby ★ **Kjeåsan** is something of a contrast. A winding road enters a tunnel, at the end of which is a wooden gate. From here you can gaze from a green pasture down to Eidfjord, but the two sisters from the farm charge a nominal entrance fee for the view. If you are unable to fit in a walk because of the weather or lack of time, then you could visit ★ **Hardangervidda Nature Centre** in Eidfjord, which provides some illuminating insights into the geology, fauna and flora of the Hardangervidda.

Map on page 44

Below and bottom: the Flåm mountain railway

LAKE VANGSVATNET

Carry on along narrow roads by the shores of the fjord, beneath mountains and through tunnels as far as **Voss** (601km/373 miles), where farming, folk dancing and handicrafts flourish. There are around 500 lakes in the region, and its rivers are famous for their salmon. **Lake Vangsvatnet**, with fishing and sailing, is the main attraction in the summer; in winter, pistes and cross-country tracks attract skiers into the surrounding mountains. Below Hangurfjell, about half an hour's walk above the town, is the ★ **Voss Folk Museum** (Mølstertunet), a folk-music gallery and collection of 16 old wooden buildings standing in a traditional form around a courtyard.

NORWAY IN A NUTSHELL

From Voss (or Bergen/Oslo) there is one departure daily for the circular excursion known as ★★★ **Norway in a Nutshell**. This runs all year and involves bus, ferry and train. It begins with a 55-minute ride on the Myrdal to Flåm railway, one of the most exciting train rides in the world. Myrdal station stands at an altitude of 865m (2,838ft), but after only 20km (12 miles) near **Flåm** you reach sea level. The train has five braking systems, each of which can bring the carriages to a halt on gradients of up to 5.5 percent. Sometimes the train stops for photographers to capture waterfalls and seemingly bottomless chasms on film.

From Flåm the trip continues by ferry to Gudvangen in the ★ **Nærøyfjord**, the narrowest and loveliest fjord in Western Norway, surrounded by mountains up to 1,800m (6,000ft) high. The last leg, from Gudvangen to Voss by bus, is gorgeous. For 1.5km (1 mile) the bus chugs its way up to the ★ **Stalheimskleivi** along the steepest road in Norway, with 13 hairpin bends.

Passengers may prefer to look over towards the **Stalheimsfossen** – this waterfall drops 240m (790ft) – than glance directly below as the edge of the road disappears beneath the bus. Cyclists wait at the bends gasping for breath. You can fully enjoy the view into the valley from the ★ **Hotel Stalheim**

JOSTEDALSBREEN GLACIER

Continue northwards to **Vangsnes** (676km/420 miles), for a ferry journey across the **Sognefjord** *(see also page 49)*. The fjord widens as it bends, and the vista is magnificent. (Alternatively you can take the ferry from Gudvangen across the **Nærøyfjord** before continuing across the Sognefjord towards Kaupanger.)

The ferry from Vangsnes docks in **Balestrand**, an idyllic village in a dramatic mountain setting; from here the road continues along the shore of the fjord before cutting inland beneath the eternal snows of the imposing ★★★ **Jostedalsbreen** glacier *(see also page 51)*.

WEST CAPE

Cross Route 6 near **Moskog**. At **Nordfjordeid**, you will have to make the decision whether or not to head for the Vestkapp (West Cape, 935km/581 miles). **Statlandet** has cliffs to the north, sandy beaches to the south and mountain ridges in the middle. This peninsula is taken by many to be the boundary between the North Sea and the North Atlantic. Currents and winds blow from all directions. Overlooking it all is the ★★ **Kjerringa** (the 'Woman') as this 400-m (1,300-ft) sheer rock of the West Cape is otherwise known, a wild plateau with a panoramic 360° view.

Star Attractions
- **Norway in a Nutshell**
- **Jostedalsbreen glacier**
- **Kjerringa**

Royal favourite
The extraordinary Sognefjord, 200km (124 miles) long and 1,300 metres (4,265 feet) deep, was a popular 19th century destination for British tourists, and the Prince of Wales visited it in 1898. Sixteen years later Kaiser Wilhelm was on holiday in Sogne when he heard of the assassination of Archduke Ferdinand, the event that triggered World War I.

Balestrand

Map
on page
44

Wild passion
Cloudberries *(multebær)* are found in mountain marshlands around late summer and early autumn. Rich in vitamin C, they are delicious in jams, desserts and liqueurs.

10: Up into the mountains

Oslo – Jotunheimen mountains – Geiranger – Ålesund (538km/334 miles)

This route offers some good detours and longer walks – through wooded hills, up the Jotunheimen mountains or along the banks of the fjords to remote viewpoints.

Oslo and, to some extent, Ålesund have cosmopolitan atmospheres but, between these two towns there tends to be a somewhat inward-looking, self-reliant attitude among the people. They have learnt to live with the vagaries of the climate and geography. The weather can change at almost every bend in the road. In June it can snow at 1,500m (5,000ft), while in the valley below the fruit trees are in flower. The people in the broad valleys are continuing to make a good living from farming, but on the fjords fruit- and vegetable growers fear increasing competition from Europe. If the first part of this tour has little of splendour, the second half more than compensates.

THE ROYAL VIEW

Dalsnibba panorama, Geiranger – note the 11 hairpin bends of Trollstigen (Troll's ladder)

The journey out of the capital runs alongside the vast **Tyrifjorden**. It is a good road (with a toll to pay) but anyone who is not in a great hurry may feel disappointed at having to rush past the woods.

Sundvollen (45km/28 miles) is the ideal spot to stretch your legs. A side road climbs for 4km (2½ miles) up the ★ Kleivstua. After a short walk you will reach the summit (487m/1,598ft), which is known as the 'Royal View'.

Star Attractions
● Jotunheimen mountains
● Lake Gjende

VALDRES FOLK MUSEUM

In **Fagernes** (186km/115 miles) the local economy is based on timber and handicrafts. The forests surrounding the area have clearly moulded the town's character, and the people's pride in their heritage is evident not just in their love of folk dancing, but also in the ★ **Valdres Folk Museum**, whose 95 old buildings house numerous fascinating collections, including the biggest collection of costumes in the country. This is the geographical and cultural heart of southern Norway.

Beyond Fagernes, the panoramic Highway 51 slowly works its way up into the mountains. The pass can be rapidly negotiated, but it would be a shame to rush this stretch. The ski resort of **Beitostølen** (224km/139 miles) is a good place to stop to enjoy clear air, snow-covered plateaux and summer skiing in bikinis or shorts.

JOTUNHEIMEN MOUNTAINS

Dating from 1878 the **Gjendesheim Turisthytte** (256km/159 miles; open 15 June–9 Oct and 15 Feb–15 Apr) is a very popular starting point for walking tours of the ★★★ **Jotunheimen mountains**. If you do not have much time to spare, then treat yourself to a day trip.

Take the boat across the deep green waters of ★★ **Lake Gjende** (984m/3,228ft above sea level) to Memurubu (overnight accommodation available, but do book ahead), then follow the signposted path beneath Beseggen (2,258m/7,408ft) back to Gjendesheim. Including the boat ride, some short sections of scrambling and a panoramic view of the lake and mountain scenery, this excursion will take about eight hours. The footsore or less energetic visitor can always take the easy path beside the shores of the lake.

Below: skiing bliss
Bottom: Jotunheimen mountains

Map on page 44

Map on page 44

👁 **National parks**
There are 25 national parks in Norway, and a current programme of countryside protection aims to have about 15 per cent of the country under the parks' protection by 2010. Large areas are dedicated to protecting special habitats and supporting biodiversity. Hunting is strictly controlled and many bears are electronically tagged.

The High Mountains

Eyes light up at the mention of **Gjendebu**, **Glitterheim** or **Spiterstulen**. Even for Norway's highest peaks, **Galdhøpiggen** (2,469m/8,100ft) and **Glittertind** (2,465m/8,087ft), you will not need axes or ropes, just warm clothing and strong thighs. **Fannaråki** on the west side of Jotunheimen National Park is more challenging, and a glacier guide is essential for negotiating the ice and the mostly safe, but steep rocks. The reward for the ascent is a view over the whole of the national park across to the Dovrefjell.

Highway 15 follows the River Otta upstream towards the fjords. From Highway 55, which branches off near **Lom** (334km/208 miles) to the south, it is possible to build in more day-long hikes. For an easy excursion, drive to the **Juvasshytta** (1,837m/6,027ft) at the foot of the Galdhøpiggen. Here, the air smells of melted snow, and in the broad ★ **Bøverdal** the cool summer breezes from the summit blend with steam rising from the wet soil.

Beyond Lom, tourist numbers start to increase as one of Norway's best-known sights is close by. But first, get a tan in the snow. The old road (Highway 258), between **Grotli** (393km/244 miles) and **Stryn**, leads up to the summer skiing centre by the ★ **Skridulaub glacier** before snaking down to Oppstryn.

Norwegian wood

Geiranger

Back in Grotli now, head north on Highway 63 to Geiranger. A few hundred metres above the pass is the ★★**Dalsnibba** panorama. You will have to pay a toll for a dusty road with sharp bends but, once there, a family photo for the album is obligatory – the view is stunning.

It takes half an hour by car to reach the fjord again, arriving at ★★★ **Geiranger** (430km/267 miles), which is probably Norway's most photographed spot. This village of around 270 inhabitants welcomes around half a million visitors a year, who come to admire the green, almost sheer cliffs and the gravity-defying farmsteads.

SUNNMØRE ALPS

From Geiranger, a suggested detour is to take the ferry to the town of **Hellesylt**, past the three famous waterfalls, 'Bride's Veil', 'Seven Sisters' and 'The Suitor', which are immortalised countless times on postcards, photos and slides, and then onto the ★★ **Sunnmøre Alps**. The peaks are popular with both climbers and walkers. From the summits, you will be able to see the foaming waters of the North Sea and snowcapped mountains. The snow on the peaks, the grey of the rocks that gradually changes into a lush green, and the turquoise of the fjords, always fun to cross, will make this excursion one to remember.

★ **Sæbø**, at the mouth of the river Bondalselva, is as colourful as a paintbox. Tranquil evenings are incredibly beautiful: boats out on the fjord head for farmhouses that cling precariously to the hillsides, the tractors have done their day's work and the salmon fishermen cast their flies – a west Norwegian idyll.

If you continue from Sæbø through the valley to Ørsta, you will join Route 6 *(see page 45)*. Back on the main route, **Valldal** (450km/280 miles) is about 5km (3 miles) east of the campsite, café and strawberry fields of **Linge**. Many people in these parts earn their living from fruit and vegetables, even managing to produce a modest crop of apricots and peaches. Tourists

Star Attractions
● **Dalsnibba**
● **Geiranger**
● **Sunnmøre Alps**

Below: Geirangersfjord
Bottom: Sæbø in winter

Map
on page
44

travelling by car often stop off and draw breath here before making for ★ **Gudbrandjuvet** and ★★ **Trollstigen** (Trolls' Ladder). The former is a terrifying gorge only 5m (16ft) wide, the latter an ascent with 11 hairpin bends. After a long run by the **Storfjord**, the landscape broadens out at **Sjøholt** (487km/303 miles), known for its furniture manufacture.

ÅLESUND

Below and bottom: aspects of Ålesund

At the port of **Ålesund** (pop. 40,000), Norway's largest fishing town, fish are sold straight from trawlers. The town was famously burned down in a fire in 1904, and Germany's Kaiser Wilhelm II sent Art-Nouveau-inspired architectural students to aid rebuilding. Exhibitions in the local museum records those events. Towers, turrets and medieval-romantic facades, often with more than a trace of Nordic mythology, give the town a harmony, which extends to the painted wooden warehouses along **Brosundet**.

Lined by Art Nouveau houses, the harbour is great for an evening stroll, and as the sun dips, the view from the ★★ **Aksla** out over the offshore islands is fabulous.

Another highlight is the ★★ **Atlanterhavsparken** (hours vary, daily feedings at 1pm), an aquarium integrated into the coastline.

11: Big city lights to the Northern Lights

Oslo – Lillehammer – Narvik – Vesterålen and Lofoten Islands – Å (1,846km/1,147 miles)

Map on page 82

This route goes from the capital to almost the end of the world, from Oslo's urban sophistication to the thinly populated Lofoten Islands – from a city where the natural world is a destination in itself, to the islands where the people depend on their natural, often harsh, environment for their living. *'Norge på langs'* ('the length of Norway'), as the route is called, is a trap for motorists, propelling them forever forwards.

The E6 and the E10 pass through unexplored regions waiting to be discovered. Trains can take you from Oslo all the way to Fauske; buses then continue the journey northward to Bodø. From there ferries leave for the Lofoten. Surprisingly, there are also numerous airports between Trondheim and Narvik, which could be used to cut these great distnaces into more manageable segments.

Regardless of your mode of transport, the goal is clear. Most people experience an inexplicable thrill and sense of achievement when they cross the *Polarsirkel* (Arctic Circle) . It marks the end of modern comforts and the beginning of the 'wild north'.

Northern Lights
The Northern Lights, or *aurora borealis*, are a metereological phenomena caused by a conflict between the Earth's magnetic field and solar winds around the poles. The energy given off by this conflict creates charged particles that cause the gases in the atmosphere to glow, producing a beautiful and eerie display of light.

LILLEHAMMER

The centre of **Lillehammer** (pop. 25,000; 180km/ 112 miles) is actually not much more than the **Storgata** pedestrian zone. Little has actually changed in this town on the northern edge of Lake Mjøsa since it flamboyantly hosted the Winter Olympics in 1994 – apart from the fact the government used US$300 million to build the ★**Lysgård ski jump**, ice-hockey arena, bobsleigh track and cross-country skiing stadium, making Lillehammer a winter wonderland. The downside is hotel and beer prices will never sink to their pre-Olympic levels again, and the queues by the ski lifts continue to grow.

Lillehammer crest

ROUTE 11 (NORTH) & 12

But during summer, the winter of 1994 seems a long way off. A blues festival is held every April, hikers still wander off into the wooded mountains to enjoy the view down over Lake Mjøsa; and tourists visit the Norges Olympiske Museum which features exhibitions on the Olympic Games from Athens 1896 to Sydney 2000.

Lillehammer's biggest attraction is still the ★★★ **Maihaugen Sandvig Collections**, an open-air museum. Nowhere else in the Gudbrandsdal is rural culture and architecture so graphically illustrated. The museum was the life work of Anders Sandvig, a dentist who came to Lillehammer in 1885 to start his own practice. He became concerned that the region's heritage was disappearing, so he started to 'collect' buildings, some 185 in all.

The buildings range from medieval to 19th and 20th century examples; Sandvig also collected some 30,000 artefacts. The museum also includes demonstrations of old skills and crafts, as well as farm life. (Maihaugvegen 7, tel: 61 28 89 00; open daily summer 10am–5pm, winter 1 Oct–16 May 11am–4pm, closed Mon). A midsummer eve celebration is held here on 23 June.

GUDBRANDSDALEN

The ★ **Gudbrandsdalen** has been on the main route to the north since the time of the sagas. The faithful followed the hillside paths on their pilgrimages to Trondheim, and for the past hundred years or so, cars and trains have sped through the valley. Farming is important here, and farm holidays are also becoming increasingly popular.

RONDANE MOUNTAINS

In the ★ **Rondane Mountains**, however, the traffic is soon forgotten. Ten peaks over

2,000m (6,560ft) tower above extremely sparse vegetation. The dry, cold climate and light sandstone restrict growth, and during the summer, the land is covered only by a greeny brown layer of lichen. The park has many marked footpaths and is home to one of the last wild reindeer herds. Even children are able to make it to the summits.

Dombås (334km/208 miles) is, at first sight, just a crossroads with cafés, petrol stations and lots of traffic, but it occupies a strategic spot between wooded mountains in the south and east, the **Reinheimen** mountains in the west and the wild and beautiful ★★ **Dovrefjell** to the north, so walkers use it as a base.

KONGSVOLD FJELLSTUE

The Dovrefjell marks the end of southern Norway. This elongated plateau has always been an obstacle on the northward journey, even for medieval pilgrims taking the King's Road to Trondheim. The ★ **Kongsvold Fjellstue**, a mountain guesthouse with a botanical garden and museum, is worth breaking your journey for, and a walk up **Snøhetta** (2,286m/7,500ft) – a towering, cone-shaped peak – is a great experience in the sun or the snow. The view from 'Norway's roof' is one of the highlights of southern Norway.

Star Attractions
● **Maihaugen Sandvig Collections**
● **Dovrefjell**

Below: the Maihaugen Sandvig Collections
Bottom: the Gudbrandsdalen

Map on page 82

PREHISTORIC HUNTING

Road and railway line follow the ★ **Gaula**, a famous salmon river, for the last few kilometres to Trondheim.

Coastal **Trondheim** (534km/332 miles; *see page 38*) is the main centre on this route. To the north, the road runs close to the fjords until it disappears into extensive birch and pine forests. **Lake Snåsavatn** beyond Steinkjer (654km/406 miles) must have been fine hunting country in prehistoric times. On its eastern shore, hunters who lived about 6,000 years ago scratched a depiction of a reindeer on to the rock, which is known as the ★★ **Bølareinen**.

Near **Grong** (736km/457 miles), many motorists branch off to the coast *(see page 90)*, as the next 170km (105 miles) have little to offer apart from dense woodland and the idyllic ★ **Lake Majavatn**, and **Børgefjell National Park**, which is angling and birdwatching country.

The Arctic Circle is now beckoning, but first the road passes through two industrial towns – **Mosjøen** (926km/575 miles), which prospered from its aluminium works, and **Mo i Rana** (1,018km/633 miles), with nearby caves and a glacier, where life revolved around iron. The steelworks of Norsk Jernverk no longer produces the same quantities it did 50 years ago, but keep an eye out for Anthony Gormley's sculpture *Havmannen*.

Below and bottom: markers at the Arctic Circle

INTO THE ARCTIC

★ **N-8242 Polarsirkelen** (1,102km/685 miles) is more than just a post office for stamp collectors. The Arctic Circle Centre here at 650m (2,132ft) above sea level is the only building for miles around. High-voltage electricity cables stretch above the barren Arctic landscape of stunted birches and old site huts.

This is the start of the ★ **Saltfjell**, whose secrets lie buried within or beneath the limestone rock. Hundreds of caves were discovered here, but only a few are open to the public. The ★ **Grønligrotta** (22km/14 miles northwest of Mo i Rana), which even has electric lights, is a popular destination and has a 20-minute tour which is suitable for families, although heavy shoes are recommended.

Finding the entrances beneath the smooth, white marble-coated rocks can take hours, but encountering the weird, underground rock formations is worth the effort.

Nordnes Camping is a good base from which to explore ★★ **Saltfjell-Svartisen National Park**. Longer river tours through this region are tasters for the journey through northern Norway: rare plants, birds of prey and reindeer between limestone rock and moorland. In addition, there are traces of Sami settlements from the 9th century set against the backdrop of the **Svartisen glacier**, which attracts many walkers (*see also page 93*).

MINING MUSEUM

Sulitjelma, 44km (27 miles) east of Fauske on Highway 830, was once a thriving mining community, but now it is slowly decaying. The supermarket staff wait for their few regular customers – Norwegians who have a summer residence in the old workers' estate of Jacobsbakken further up in the woods – and for travellers who visit the **mining museum** and the smelting plant, which was decommissioned in 1991.

Local employment prospects look bleak, as does the immediate future for the nearby lake, where all plant life and fish were destroyed by industrial pollution.

Star Attractions
● **Bølareinen**
● **Saltfjell-Svartisen National Park**

Below: arctic flora, Saltfjell-Svartisen National Park
Bottom: on the Steigen coast

Map
on page
82

Train trip
A 'tourist train' from Narvik to the Swedish border runs in the summer. This three-hour guided trip offers photo opportunities and the chance to buy Sami souvenirs.

STEIGEN

Beyond **Fauske** (1,202km/747 miles), tunnels channel tourists northward. If you are not in a hurry, take the 8-km (5-mile) Steigen tunnel, which leads off into an Arctic fairyland to the west of the E6. The view from ★★ **Steigen** over to the Lofot wall is worth the detour alone (about 60km/37 miles one way). Whether it soothes or excites will depend on the dramatic colour of sea and sky. With steep cliffs and sandy beaches blending into the Vestfjord, the view is breathtakingly beautiful.

The people of Steigen are proud that their part of the world was inhabited by the Vikings, and their ancestors and burial mounds, memorial stones and settlements testify to the Viking's presence here. A parsonage dates from 1886 and the huge fortress at **Bø**, which the Germans built to defend Narvik, is now a tourist attraction.

NARVIK

The world of Knut Hamsun starts beyond ★ **Kråkmotinden**. In a farmhouse in **Kråkmo** at the foot of the mountain, which is shaped like a molar tooth, Knut Hamsun wrote novels and the first chapter of his work, *Growth of the Soil*. **Oppeid**, situated 14km (9 miles) to the west of the E6, has something different to offer apart from memories of Norway's most famous novelist. The earth closet with two sets of three seats, now in the local history museum, is proof that even in rural Norway, a class divide existed. The Nordland artist Karl Erik Harr has a gallery in ★ **Tranøy** to the north of Hamarøy. The lighthouse here is now a guesthouse.

Narvik (pop. 18,500; 1,445km/898 miles) has its own chapter in European history. A stroll around the town ought to begin at the vast iron ore loading terminal and end at the **Ofotbanen** railway line – this terminus is only 45 minutes away from the Swedish border and two hours from the town of Kiruna. The railway was built in the 1890s, so that iron ore could be shipped from the ice-free harbour, hence its strategic importance during World War II. Taken once by

Narvik signpost

the Germans and won back by the Allies who were then forced to withdraw, the town has an excellent ★ **War Memorial Museum**, which illustrates five years of Nazi occupation during the war. Only the ruins of the old town remain. Modern Narvik is an important commercial centre and a busy winter sports resort, but it offers little beauty apart from the surrounding mountains. Take the cable car to view the fjord and mountains.

Star Attractions
● Steigen
● Vesterålen and
Lofoten Islands

VESTERÅLEN AND LOFOTEN ISLANDS

The route now heads west to explore the ★★★ **Vesterålen** and **Lofoten Islands**. At the bridge across to **Sortland** (1,646km/1,023 miles), you face a difficult choice: every little road leads to the sea, every fjord is, in the opinion of the locals, a gem, and in every fishing village there are *rorbuer* (fishermen's cabins) as well as old boat and net stores, which are now hired out as holiday cabins.

Below: Lofoten birdlife
Bottom: the bridge to Sortland

The Vesterålen and Lofoten were popular summer hideaways, even during the 19th century, when transport was far less sophisticated than it is today. The unspoilt natural environment and long hours of sunlight are the attractions here. The pointed peaks of the mountains reflecting in the clear waters of the sea have proved irresistible to many poets, musicians and painters.

Map on page 82

Whale safaris
Trips for whale safaris leave from Andenes, Stø and Nyksund and last around four hours. If you don't see a whale, you get a second, free trip. It's best to book in advance (tel: 76 11 56 00).

Below: Nyksund
Bottom: Svolvær

ANDENES

★ **Andenes**, in the north of the **Vesterålen** island of Andøya, is also a place of inspiration, and the popularity of the whale safaris that take place every day in the summer *(see panel on left)* does not derive entirely from the grey whale – catching a glimpse of one is almost guaranteed anyway. The houses in Andenes testify to the one-time prosperity of the fishermen in this former whaling community, and the **Polar Museum** gives a glimpse of its history.

At the northwestern tip of the neighbouring island, the old fishing village of **Nyksund** is just one of several fishing villages in northern Norway that have been deserted. The North Atlantic has torn holes in the abandoned houses, but among the remains, idealists have sought to save one or two *rorbuer* (fishermen's cabins) from collapse. Groups of young people from many European countries have attempted to revive the village to create an international meeting place.

FISHING SETTLEMENTS

The mountain known as the 'Svolvær goat' greets visitors to the **Lofotens** from afar. This symbol for the town of **Svolvær** (pop. 4,150; 1,720km/1,069 miles), which is the capital of the 18 islands, is one of many peaks on the island that really is as steep as it looks. Svolvær is developing a reputation as something of an artists' colony, and it is sometimes possible to watch them at work in the Artists' House. Many of the island's highlights can be reached from here, either by road or by boat. There is a ferry across to ★★ **Skrova**, for example, whose inhabitants (and their ancestors) have earned their living from the whale for many years, and who are in their element when regaling outsiders about life in the old days when the quotas were not so tight and celebrations marked the return of the whalers.

Between February and April, ★ **Kabelvåg** (pop. 1,600) is the undisputed fishing capital of northern Norway. Up to 10,000 vessels make for the Vestfjord during these months. The colourful

Lofotfiske, annual cod-fishing event, is held in late March. The town's **★★ Vågan church** is the biggest wooden church north of Trondheim.

Henningsvær, **Napp**, **Nusfjord** and **Stamsund** on the east side of Lofotens are all fishing villages celebrated for their beautiful, restored *rorbuer*, some of which are up to 150 years old; they also all offer some tempting fish restaurants and cafés. This area was an important Viking settlement as long ago as AD 600. A reconstruction of a Viking farmhouse and displays on everyday life can be seen in the **★★ Lofotr Viking Museum** in Borg (tel: 76 08 49 00; open summer 10am–6pm, winter and autumn 1–3pm). Near **★★ Hamnøy** (1,833km/ 1,139 miles) beneath the pointed peak of the **★ Olstind**, you will cross the last of the countless bridges on the Lofoten Islands. In Hamnøy, one of the oldest Lofoten villages, fish are left to dry on three-legged stands. Fishing vessels are tied up at the quay, beside the fish market and cabins.

The road ends at **Å** (1,846km/1,147 miles), named after the last letter of the Norwegian alphabet. Now all that remains is the walk to the **★ Lofotoden** at the southern tip of the islands. The view from here over two of the islands is delightful. Many people get off the ferry from **Moskenes** at the outlying islands of **Værøy** or **Røst** or else return to the mainland in Bodø *(see page 94)*, the end of the Nordland railway line.

Star Attractions
● **Skrova**
● **Vågan church**
● **Lofotr Viking Museum**
● **Hamnøy**

Below: Henningsvær
Bottom: Nusfjord

Map
on page
82

Ice fishing

Winter is the time to come skiing in Norway, but why not try fishing, too? Ice is no deterrent to Norwegians, who require only a baited line or a short pole and line, warm clothing and lots of patience. Holes in the ice must be cut by hand as motor devices are prohibited.

12: Helgeland – islands, meadows and glaciers

Grong – Brønnøysund – Sandnessjøen – Bodø (560km/348 miles)

A warming Gulf Stream, icy glaciers, rock formations that defy description, 12,000 islands, sandy beaches and lush meadows, mountain hikes and deep-sea fishing – a veritable treasure-trove for historians and bird-lovers, and all of it close to the Arctic Circle. This route along Highway 17 takes you to one of the most beautiful stretches of road in Europe.

FERRIES AND THE HIGHWAY

To complete this route, you will have to make several ferry crossings, and the journey needs to be carefully planned, not least because of the cost. You can reach the starting point in a number of ways. Either leave the E6 in Steinkjer or else go as far as Grong and then branch off to the west. Bus or train travellers can take the Nordlandsbanen to Grong but, with so many ferry crossings to make, how they continue will depend on the amount of time and money available. Owners of ferry passes can save a substantial amount of money. These passes are available at all tourist information offices by Highway 17 and by the E6 in Nordland. The main ferry crossings and schedules are as follows:

Fishing haven beside Highway 17

Holm–Vennesund, 20 minutes, 15 crossings daily (6.25am–10.25pm); Horn–Anddaslvåg, 15 minutes, 11 crossings daily (6am–10pm); Forvik– Tjøtta, 60 minutes, 7 crossings daily (6.55am– 9.30pm); Levang–Nesna, 20 minutes, 14 crossings daily (6.25am–11.35pm); Kilboghamm– Jektvik, 60 minutes, 5 crossings daily (8.30am–9.30pm); Ågskardet– Forøy, 10 minutes, 12 crossings daily (5.40am–10.05pm).

GRONG

Grong (pop. 2,500) is a popular rendezvous for fishermen, as the **Namsen** river is renowned for its salmon – and also for the cost of a fishing licence. It is cheaper to fish near the ★ **Tømmeråsfossen**. The salmon jump here attracts many visitors, but some patience is required if you want to see the fish take to the air.

From Grong, take Highway 760 westwards towards Namsos, turning right along Highway 17 by the Bjøra Bridge after 20km (12 miles). The traffic in these parts seems to flow as gently as the streams and rivers. **Nordlandskorsen** (101km/63 miles) marks the start of a region which has a total coastline of 57,000km (35,500 miles).

Star Attraction
● Torghatten

TORGHATTEN

Brønnøysund (pop. 4,000; 190km/118 miles) is a municipality made up of over 2,000 islands, one of which, **Torget**, features prominently in Norse mythology. The hat-shaped ★★ **Torghatten**, the island's mountain, is pierced at a level of 160m (525ft) by a great hole more than 40m (130ft) high. Legend has it that the hole was made by a horseman, thwarted in love, who shot an arrow at his lady, the Maid of Leka. Just in time, the mountain king of Sømnafjellet saw what was happening and threw his hat in the air to intercept the arrow. Emperors, kings and, more recently, less illustrious visitors have come to examine the curiosity, which is actually quite easy to explore,

Below: Torghatten
Bottom: Brønnøysund

Map
on page
82

A mark of respect
The poet Petter Dass was so
well known in Norway that
after his death in 1708, most ships
carried a black patch on their sails.
The practice continued for a century.

as it's only a 30-minute scramble up the rocky
path from the road.

★★ **Forvik/Vevelstad** (218km/135 miles) is
typical of Helgeland. The history of the village
goes back many thousands of years, as shown
by rock drawings from the Iron Age and a Stone
Age settlement on the island of ★ **Hamnøy**, more
and more of which is being exposed by drifting
sands. The church and even the guesthouse in the
village were built about 200 years ago, and it's
certainly worth breaking your journey to visit the
Handelstedet Forvik. Built in 1792, the guesthouse enjoys a fabulous view of the fjord, out
towards the imposing peaks of the 'Seven Sisters'.

THE SEVEN SISTERS

Each of these peaks, which range between 910m
(2,985ft) and 1,072m (3,517ft), can be climbed
without special equipment and along marked footpaths. The current record for all seven is just under
four hours. According to a Norse saga, these
seven peaks were once the daughters of the king
of Sulitjelma. Pursued by the 'horseman', they
sat down here exhausted and turned to stone when
sunlight reached the earth.

The short section of road between **Tjøtta** and
Sandnessjøen runs through the best farmland in
northern Norway, and there can hardly be a finer

The Seven Sisters

sandy beach north of the Alps than the one here. Its water is crystal clear, the sea scattered with countless islands and, almost adjacent, are tall rock formations, whose shadows spread across the azure blue waters in the late evening.

ALSTAHAUG

★★ **Alstahaug** (237km/147 miles) was the home of Petter Dass (1647–1707), a priest and the only celebrated Norwegian poet of the 17th century. He earned his living from selling fish, but also wrote psalms and poems. *Trumpets of the Nordland* is a declaration of his love of the Seven Sisters. The church, the **Petter Dass Museum** and the red-washed houses in the town are all worth visiting.

The Helgelanders are particularly proud of the ★ **phallic symbol** on the island of **Dønna** off **Sandnessjøen**, of the 1,065-m (3,494-ft) long Helgeland Bridge, which sways in strong winds, of the memorial stones, the old farmsteads and the modern fish farms. Every island is worth a visit, but nowhere has such broad sandy beaches and such a magnificent panoramic view as **Dønna**, nowhere as much fish as **Herøy**, nowhere as many puffins as ★★ **Lovund**.

Towering above them all on the island of **Hestmona** is the 568-m (1,863-ft) high ★★ **Hestmannen**, the 'horseman', the warrior whose arrow wreaked so much havoc – but who then turned to stone himself. An ascent takes just under two hours and, apart from a short section by a steep drop, is really quite easy.

SVARTISEN GLACIER

While waiting for ferries at **Kilboghamn** (377km/234 miles), try the pleasant 2-km (1¼-mile) walk to ★ **Stensland** by the Melfjord; when the boat finally moors at the foot of the **Værangfjord**, it is goodbye to the flat, green coastal strip. This is ★★ **Svartisen glacier** country. The Svartisen is not only the second largest glacier in Norway (after Jostedalsbreen, *see page*

Star Attractions
● Forvik/Vevelstad
● Alstahaug
● Lovund
● Hestmannen
● Svartisen glacier

Below: Svartisen glacier and (bottom) a nearby ferry

Map on page 82

51), covering an area of 370 sq km (143 sq miles), but has the added distinction of being the lowest-lying glacier on the European mainland, reaching down to within 20m (65ft) of sea level. The section of the route from **Forøy** (392km/243 miles) to **Glomfjord** (427km/265 miles) is absolutely perfect for an overnight stay, a glacier walk and a trip on the ★★ **Holandsfjord** as far as **Engabreen**.

Nestling beneath the Nordland mountains, ★ **Ørnes** (446km/277 miles) and **Grimstad** are idyllic ports which look out over the sea. Fishing, walking, boat trips and mountain climbing – there is so much for the energetic visitor to do. Before you leave this region, pay a visit to the ★ **Saltstraumen** (536km/333 miles); stand on the bridge across the **Saltfjord** and watch the impressive tidal ebb and flow within the inner fjord. This is the most powerful maelstrom in the world: look down and it will seem as if you are being sucked along by vast quantities of water. To find out more about the mythology related to the maelstrom, visit the ★ **Saltstraumen Adventure Centre**.

Bodø (560km/348 miles; ferries to the Lofoten Islands) is an attractive town and this scenic tour's final port of call. The town is home to the Norsk Luftfartssenter (Norwegian Aviation Centre; open all year; entrance charge), which has a selection of planes and a flight simulator.

Below: the Norwegian Aviation Centre
Bottom: Bodø

13: The far north

Narvik – Alta – Olderfjord – Lakselv – Tana Bru – Karasjok (1,277km/793 miles without detours)

Many people drive up to the North Cape, see the midnight sun if they are lucky, and then drive off.

The region to the north of the Arctic Circle is vast. It comprises the Finnmarksvidda, a plateau of seemingly infinite dimensions, particularly during the long, black winter nights, the jagged Arctic Ocean coastline and scores of tiny places, where buildings and inhabitants alike still bear the scars of the scorched earth policy employed by the Germans in World War II. The struggle between the warring nations for the iron ore harbour of Narvik in 1940 left large parts of the town and outlying area in ruins.

Then there is the extreme climate. It can get really warm, sometimes above 25°C (77°F), and then giant mosquitoes come out to bite. Sometimes as early as October, the Northern Lights appear above the icy cold *vidda*.

ARCTIC TRAVEL

The Hurtigruten coastal ship fleet is an important link between the northern coastal towns and the south, but what about the villages of the interior? What use are buses and cars when there is deep snow on the ground? Snow scooters and helicopters are vital in these never-ending expanses of the frozen north. Whether you are travelling by car or by bus, the distances involved here are huge; they are, however, worth covering if you have time to spare and want to see some spectacular scenery.

SENJA

Almost as soon as you have begun the long trip northwards along the E6 from Narvik, an opportunity for a detour presents itself. Having visited the islands of Lofoten and Vesterålen *(see page 87)*, you can now consider making for another large island. Turn left in **Fossbakken** (61km/38 miles) to the beautiful northwestern

Sami view
'I've been fighting this feeling of being inferior to Norwegian or western people, and my voice got stronger as I decided I wouldn't let anyone oppress me and that I have a value as Sami. Western culture makes a distance between you and your body or heart. In Sami culture you think of everything as a whole' – singer Mari Boine.

Sami woman

Map below

island of ★★ **Senja**, the second largest island in Norway. The Gulf Stream is responsible for the lush vegetation, and the **Ånderdalen National Park** in the interior contains a cross-section of Senja's rich flora.

Fish dish
Puffins take around 10 fish back to their nest on each fishing trip. The record sighted is 62 in one beak, which is adapted to hold fish in quantity. A raspy tongue holds each fish against spines on its palate, enabling the puffin to open its beak to catch more.

Hungry puffin

LYNGEN MOUNTAINS

At **Nordkjosbotn** (182km/113 miles) the most direct route north is to continue along the E6 via **Skibotn**, following the eastern shore of the Lyngenfjord, with its panoramic views of the ★★ **Lyngen mountains** across the water. The sight of the pointed, snowcapped peaks of the Lyngens would give any climber itchy feet; in fact there is no shortage of mountains in these parts, but nowhere else is the combination of mountain and fjord more spectacular. An attractive alternative route to see the Lyngens at closer quarters is to take the E8 towards Tromsø *(see page 41)*, turning right 25km (16 miles) before the town, along Highway 91 through the Breivik Valley. At the end of this road, a ferry bridges the **Ullsfjord** to Svensby. Then drive to ★ **Lyngseidet**, where you can catch another ferry to **Olderdalen** on the E6.

Karvik (394km/245 miles) marks the end of one of the most beautiful sections of the E6. The view from the summit of the 402-m (1,319-ft) high ★★ **Kvænangsfjellet** across to the **Øksfjord**

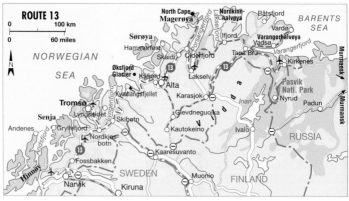

ROUTE 13

0   100 km
0   60 miles

N

NORWEGIAN SEA

BARENTS SEA

North Cape
Magerøya
Nordkinn-halvøya
Båtsfjord
Vardø
Varangerhalvøya
Vadsø
Sørøya
Hammerfest
Skaidi
Olderfjord
Ifjord
Tana Bru
Varangerfjord
Kirkenes

Øksfjord Glacier
Kåfjord
Alta
Lakselv
Murmansk

Tromsø
Kvænangsfjellet
Karasjok
Pasvik Natl. Park
Nyrud
Padun

Senja
Lyngseidet
Skibotn
Glevdneguolka
Inari
Murmansk

Andenes
Gryllefjord
Nordkjosbotn
Kautokeino
Ivalo
RUSSIA

Fossbakken
Kaaresuvanto
SWEDEN
Muonio
FINLAND

Narvik
Kiruna

glacier to the northwest is quite spellbinding, even when there is a strong icy wind blowing.

Kåfjord (pop. 150; 499km/310 miles) was once an important mining town, and between 1826 and 1878 had almost as many inhabitants as Hammerfest. During World War II, the Germans attempted to hide the battleship *Tirpitz* in the fjord outside the village, but it was discovered by British submarines. On 22 September 1943 when the Germans tried to move the vessel to Tromsø, it was attacked by British planes and badly damaged. It was finally sunk on 12 November 1944.

HJEMMELUFT ROCK CARVINGS

Rebuilt after World War II, **Alta** (pop. 17,000; 524km/316 miles) is the main educational centre for the province of Finnmark, but is still, strictly speaking, not a town. The place is a melting pot of Norwegian and Sami culture. Both communities are proud of ★★★ **Hjemmeluft**, the largest collection of rock carvings north of Italy, and a UNESCO World Heritage Site. So far, some 4,000 carvings have been discovered, with some said to be 6,200 years old. The acclaimed ★★ **Alta Museum**, perched on the edge of the fjord, has fine examples of rock art on show.

It is worth making the 58-km (36-mile) detour from **Skaidi** to ★ **Hammerfest**, not just because it is the most northerly town in the world, but also for the journey along Highway 94. You are unlikely to forget the sight of the salmon-rich **Repparfjordelva** and ★ **Kvalsund**, where reindeer venture right to the edge of the road.

NORTH CAPE

Up here the water is deep blue, and a walk on the island of **Kvaløya** makes a welcome change from the long road to ★★★ **North Cape**. To reach this desolate spot at 71°N, leave **Olderfjord** (627km/390 miles) and keep going towards the island of **Magerøya**, connected to the mainland by a bridge and tunnel. Opened in 1999, this is the northernmost road tunnel in the world; 7km

Star Attractions
● Senja
● Lyngen mountains
● Kvænangsfjellet
● Hjemmeluft
● Alta Museum
● North Cape

Below: rock art at Alta
Bottom: North Cape

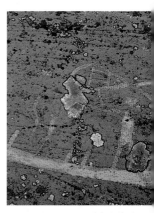

Map on page 96

A lot of Belloni

The phrase 'land of the midnight sun' was coined by the French-American explorer Paul Belloni du Chaillu (1835–1903), who published a travelogue by the same title in 1881 after travelling extensively in northern Europe.

(4 miles) long, and 212m (695ft) deep, it has become a tourist attraction in its own right.

Should the weather be poor, you can see the famous North Cape cliffs through the windows of ★ **North Cape Hall**, which is built within a cliff, where there are also exhibitions, multivision shows, a chapel, restaurants, a post office and souvenir shops. A visit to the fishing harbour at ★★ **Skarsvåg** may well prove more interesting. The cape is just around the corner, but to sit above the houses on the hard lichen and to survey the village and the sea is pure bliss.

FINNMARK

At **Lakselv** (690km/429 miles) you have a choice of routes: if it is cool and wet, you're best advised to take the E6 directly to the main Sami town of **Karasjok** (pop. 2,900; 74km/46 miles from Lakselv). The midges are not too great a problem here, and it is easier to get close to the people and the countryside than if you take the alternative route suggested below. Pay a visit to the ★★ **church**, the ★★ **Sami museum**, the ★ **Sápmi theme park**, which opened in 2002 and explores different aspects of Sami culture and tradition, and the **Samegammen** restaurant.

If summer has reached Finnmark, it is better to take Highway 98/E75 to **Tana Bru** and the

Resident Sami

'land by the Arctic Ocean' on the east and west shore of the **Tanafjord**.

Highway 98/E75 passes through the provincial capital of **Vadsø** (pop. 6,200) before reaching the Arctic Ocean at ★★ **Vardø** (pop. 2,650). Vardø obtained its municipal charter in 1789, but was founded as a fortress town in 1309.

Before setting out on the long journey by the banks of the river Tana and the Finnish border towards Karasjok, it is worth taking a detour to **Kirkenes**, and on a further 64km (40 miles) to the border post at ★★ **Grense Jakobselv** (410km/255 miles there and back). Time-consuming it may be, but it is interesting to observe at close quarters this multi-cultural community in which Russians from across the border to the east also play a part. There are often open-air flea markets.

With the Barents Sea to the northeast, Kirkenes is the last and northernmost port for the Hurtigruten (fleet of ships travelling along the northern coast). An increasing number of passengers are discovering the magnificent scenery to the south of the town, including the valleys, lakes, waterfalls and forests of the ★★ **Pasvik National Park**, in the triangle of land bordered by Finland and Russia. This is a paradise for birds, elks and wolverines, not to mention Norway's biggest bear colony. It would not be unusual to come face to face with a bear, so if you hear the whistling noise of one feeding, make a slow retreat. Bears do not like people, but if you flee in panic then the animal may give chase. The Pasvik National Park Centre (open summer) has exhibitions on local nature and culture.

Follow the E6 north and then head south along the Tana river to **Karasjok** (1,081km/672 miles). After a further 93km (58 miles), Highway 93 forks north to Alta, thus completing the circuit (1,277km/793 miles). However, if you go south on the same road, towards the Finnish border, you will arrive in **Kautokeino**, the largest Sami community in the country and the centre of Sami education. The **Kulturhus** has the only Sami theatre in Norway, and the museum's indoor and outdoor exhibits show Sami life in old Kautokeino.

Star Attractions
● Skarsvåg
● Sami church and museum
● Vardø
● Grense Jakobselv
● Pasvik National Park

Below: national park elk
Bottom: the midnight sun

A Rich Heritage

Traces of Norwegian culture date right back to prehistoric times, when the coastal hunting and fishing communities, such as those at Alta in Finnmark, created enormous rock carvings depicting their prey. During the Bronze Age, carvings became highly stylised, probably representing the fertility symbols of an early form of religion.

VIKING RULE

The end of the 8th century to the mid-11th century was the era of the Vikings, who not only plundered distant shores, but also left their mark on European culture in the areas they settled. The creativity of the Vikings is manifest in the design of their ships. Works of art in their own right, they had their prows embellished with fine wood-carving. But the Vikings were not the only ones to make their mark. The transition to Christianity during the 11th and 12th centuries fostered a cultural exchange that set an indelible stamp on the traditions of the country.

This first period of economic prosperity was followed by a '400-year sleep'. This rather sour description of Danish rule between 1397 and 1814 stems from the fact the Norwegians were robbed of their own national identity. 'Culture' was something that the overlords brought with them from foreign capitals. But with much of the inland population almost completely isolated until the 20th century, Norway was able to preserve many elements of its old folk heritage. This heritage was rediscovered during the age of Romanticism of the mid-19th century. The revival was spearheaded by a variety of writers, painters and musicians, some of whom, such as Ibsen and Grieg, achieved world-wide fame.

MODERN AGE

During the 1990s, the cultural achievements of the 'land of the midnight sun' found wider expression abroad. The Winter Olympics in Lillehammer in

Opposite: stave church, Borgund
Below: rock paintings
Bottom: Viking influence

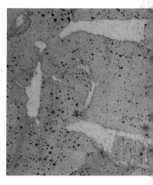

1994 played their part in boosting Norway's profile. And today, the country's arts and crafts continue to be inspired by finds from the Viking age, by the culture of the Sami, as well as by advanced schools of art and design.

Architecture

Below: A typical hytter
Bottom: decorated interior

By the 12th century, Christianity had supplanted the Viking aristocracy as the prime patron of the arts, and the stave church became the major outlet of woodcarving as an art form. These early wooden churches were mostly built in a 100-year period from 1150 to 1250. Only 29 stave churches remain, with those at Heddal, Borgund and Urnes among the best known. But they serve as fascinating examples of an architectural style that is technically well thought out and artistically varied. What they all have in common is an outer shell made with massive timber uprights (staves) buried in the ground. The surviving stave churches have small, simple interiors with a nave and a narrow chancel. Every church has a different pattern for its windows, door and internal layout. The ornamentation on the portal is often quite delicate, with motifs (such as the animal heads of Norse mythology) derived from the pagan Viking era as well as from Christianity.

Norwegian medieval artisans not only left their mark on churches, but also on the portals, window surrounds and other details of farm buildings. Even today, timber is the preferred building material of Norwegian architects, and medieval design features are often visible, such as in timber *hytter* (huts or country cottages).

Peasant artisans also used paint to decorate carved building details and household furnishings and implements, although no very early examples of this remain. Such rustic painting, often misleadingly termed 'rose painting', includes flowery designs, but also geometric figures, portraits and occasional landscapes. The relative isolation of the valleys meant that each one had its own individual style, although from the 18th century, local artisans were influenced by the influx of the professional classes into the rural areas. As with woodcarving, rustic painting is still practised.

Painting and sculpture

Another aspect of Norway's modern cultural history is evident in painting: anyone with any talent went abroad. In the absence of any native traditions, the Romantics Adolph Tidemand (1814–76), Hans Gude (1825–1903) and J.C. Dahl (1788–1857) learnt their skills and taught in Germany. Their paintings of landscapes and themes from rural life represent the emotional and artistic expression of a new sense of pride and confidence in an emerging nation.

Edvard Munch (1863–1944) was one of the first artists to distance himself from Romanticism. Many regard him now as one of the fathers of Expressionism and a pioneer in the development of graphic art. He spent many years of his life in Berlin, and during his lifetime was better known in Germany than in his native country. Death and desolation are the recurring themes most strongly expressed in his works, *The Scream* (1893), *The Kiss* (1897) and *The Vampire* (1893). Displays in the Munch Museum and the National Gallery in Oslo, as well as the Rasmus Meyer Collection in Bergen, provide good insight into his work. The principal exponents of contemporary

Below: statue by Vigeland
Bottom: a version of Munch's famous work, The Scream, *outside the student 'Blitz' house in Oslo*

Norwegian art include Jakob Weidemann with his abstract portrayals of nature, the figurative Expressionist Franz Widerberg, and the controversial Odd Nerdrum, who tends towards Neoromanticism in his mythology-influenced work.

The Norwegian sculptor, Gustav Vigeland (1869–1943), also frequently headed south in search of fellow artists and inspiration. Regarded as a genius by many art critics, Vigeland stood out among his Norwegian contemporaries, but this recognition was insufficient for him to make a living from his art. As a result, in 1921 Vigeland offered his life's works to the city of Oslo and in return received a studio and a park. Vigelandspark, in Oslo's west, is now one of the most popular destinations in Norway, and the spectacular statues displayed within are world famous. His former studio is now an excellent museum.

Literature

Retaining Norway's cultural heritage was an important motive for Jørgen Moe and Peter Asbjørnsen. In 1852, they produced the first complete collection of Norse myths. Henrik Ibsen (1828–1906) wrote his first major historical drama, *Kongsemnerne* (The Pretenders), in 1863, but he wrote the bulk of his work while living abroad, mainly in Rome, Dresden and Munich. His poetic drama

Below: Amalie Skram
Bottom: theatre in Stiklestad

Brand (1866), which established his international reputation, was a spirited indictment of Norwegian authority, while *Peer Gynt* (1867) was a reworking of national legends. Ibsen went on to write plays of realism and social issues, such as *Ghosts* (1881), which revolutionised European drama.

In the second half of the 19th century, two women aroused interest in Scandinavian literary circles. *Amtmandens Døtre* (The Magistrate's Daughter) by realist Camilla Collett (1813–95), published in 1854, raised serious issues about women's rights. Collett's attacks on the male-dominated society were continued by Amalie Skram (1846–1905), who created controversy throughout Scandinavia. Her work *Under Observation* (1895) is considered one of the first feminist novels.

The novelist Knut Hamsun (1859–1952) was a Nazi sympathiser, so at the end of World War II his works were reappraised in a different light. Nevertheless, he was the first Norwegian to find a readership abroad and his works are still widely appreciated. His chilling novel *Hunger* (1890) is an exposé of the abuses of bourgeois Swedish rule, while his masterpiece, *The Growth of the Soil* (1917), reflects a deep love of nature and concern for the effects of material conditions on the individual spirit. Hamsun was awarded the Nobel Prize in literature in 1920.

Few recent individual works have had lasting success abroad. Novelists Knud Faldbakken, Gerd Brantenberg, Herbjørg Wassmo and Ingvar Ambjørnsen and crime writer Gunnar Staalesen have been translated from Norwegian, but they have a long way to go before they can match names such as Hamsun and Ibsen. Norwegian children's and teenage literature is enjoying acclaim with Anne Vestly, Torbjørn Egner and Jostein Gaarder – author of the best-selling *Sophie's World* – among the leading names.

> **Folk tales**
> Norway has a long tradition of folk tales, which were often used by clergymen as a means of teaching morality. In the mid-19th century Jørgen Moe and Peter Asbjørnsen collected and compiled these tales for publication. The illustrated editions of the books depicted trolls for the first time.

Peer Gynt, *Ibsen's reworking of a legend, depicted here by P.N. Arboe*

Music

The past has a greater influence on Norwegian music than on its literature. Folk music is still a source of inspiration for many composers, but

Below: Mari Boine
Bottom: Edvard Grieg

modern adaptations render such traditional styles of music accessible to a wide and even a young audience. The 19th century violinist Ole Bull was the main instigator here. Edvard Grieg (1843–1907) is undoubtedly the country's most celebrated composer. His life and work reflect the two main elements of Norwegian culture: many of his compositions recall folk-music themes, some dating from the early Middle Ages, and he spent many years abroad before gaining recognition in his own country. While living in Copenhagen, Grieg came into contact with Niels Gade and Hans Christian Andersen, and it was under their influence that he evolved from a German-trained romanticist into a strongly national Norwegian composer.

Thanks to today's variety of musical techniques, Grieg's descendants have gained recognition. Saxophonist Jan Garbarek and singer Mari Boine often choose Sami songs or *joiks* as the basis for their compositions, while bassist Arild Andersen integrates peasant folk music into his pieces. The festivals in Molde, Kongsberg, Stravanger and Voss are now important dates in the jazz fan's calendar.

Pop bands A-Ha and Røyksopp and the symphony orchestras from Oslo and Bergen are very much at home in international concert halls. The International Music Festival that takes place in Bergen at the end of May is now a well-established event and a showcase for emerging talent.

Festivals and Events

January: Northern Lights Festival in Tromsø. Classical and contemporary music. Lillehammer Jazz Festival.

February: Røros Fair, held since 1854. Kristiansund Opera Festival.

March: Narvik Winter Festival, with music, dance and carnivals, including steam engine trips. The Birkebeinerrennet cross-country ski race between Rena and Lillehammer.

Palm Sunday: Vossajazz in the western town of Voss marks the start of the jazz season.

Easter: Sami in Kautokeino and Karasjok with five days of music, markets and reindeer racing.

May: Processions on 17 May (Independence Day) commemorate the signing of the Norwegian constitution on that day in 1814. The country's main music festival in Bergen lasts for two weeks at the end of May. Bergen Gay Pride Festival.

Mid-June: The North Cape Festival in Honningsvag is the world's northernmost festival. The Norwegian Wood Rock Festival attracts international bands, held in Oslo.

End June: Historic drama, folklore, ballet and art exhibitions for Harstad's festival of North Norway.

July: St Olav amateur play in Stiklestad/Verdal, near Trondheim. Quart Rock Festival, Kristiansand.

Mid to end July: International Jazz Festival, one of Europe's oldest, in Molde.

July/August: Kongsberg International Jazz Festival in the old mining town. Melbu, Vesterålen Islands international music festival.

Beginning August: Risør Wooden Boat Festival on the south coast. Chamber music festival, six-day jazz festival and Øya Rock Festival in Oslo.

Mid-August: International Chamber Music Festival in Stavanger. Norwegian Film Festival in Haugesund. Ibsen Festival in Oslo. Telemark International Folk Festival in Bø, featuring Norwegian and world artists. Varanger Festival in Vadsø features jazz concerts and jazz cruises.

October: Ultima Contemporary Music Festival in Oslo. Lillehammer Rhythm and Roots Festival.

Below: folk dancing, Molde
Bottom: the annual St Olav play, Stiklestad/Verdal

FOOD AND DRINK

'Everything that is genuinely Norwegian, and is therefore simple, has lost its appeal… Here we are very attached to our own Norwegian, barbarian habits. We are not cannibals… but we drink *akevitt* (schnapps), eat brown cheese and love partially fermented, salted trout…' Food in Norway is much better than this quote, taken from *Scenes from Life in the Lion Salon*, published in Oslo in 1848, implies. But the sentiment the book conveys, as an attack on city life and the growing enthusiasm for foreign food, still holds true for many Norwegians.

TRADITIONAL DISHES

In the larger towns if you want fast food then the choice is between a restaurant serving continental-style food such as lasagne or quiche or a *gatekjøkken* – takeaway street kitchen. In country areas, cooks take the view that locals and visitors should be spoilt with traditional Norwegian fare. The most popular dish is *kjøttkaker* (meat-cakes), but *røkepølse* (smoked sausage) and boiled lamb with mashed root vegetables are other favourites.

You should certainly sample some of the different fish dishes, such as *lutefisk*, and try to acquire an invitation to a Norwegian banquet. Here you can expect to find traditional fishermen's and farmer's dishes with regional differences in cuisine in evidence.

For festive meals, genuine Norwegian food will be served, while meals during the working week have become more international. Only the Norwegian packed lunch is sacred. It will consist of two or three slices of bread with goat's cheese, mutton salami (*fårepølse*) and low-fat white cheese.

But *kjøttkaker* remain first choice for many Norwegians' midday meal,

preferably served with gravy and mushy peas. Second choice will be pollock or cod fillet, possibly followed by rice pudding, a favourite dessert for Saturday lunch. Include the delicious fishcakes (*fiskekaker*), the dried flat loaf (*flatbrød*) and genuine Norwegian *lapskaus* (meat-and-vegetable stew) and that just about completes the picture: traditional dishes with ingredients from land and sea.

Elk steaks

Hunting is still a popular pursuit in Scandinavia and in the far north some Sami live from breeding reindeer. If you get the chance on your journey up to the North Cape, do try elk steaks, reindeer steaks or even reindeer strips (*finnebiff*), the latter being the result of an ancient method of preserving reindeer meat. Any remaining flesh is scraped from the bones and stored in portions in the snow.

HEALTHY EATING

A well-balanced diet is an important feature of Norwegian cooking. However, the cold climate is not partial to low-fat food. When it comes to special meals for special occasions, the fat content invariably rises. The simple *rømmegrøt*, for example, is a porridge made from fatty sour cream, and it can have the same effect on the waistline as rice pudding. Although sometimes saved for Easter or Christmas, it is served just about everywhere on 17 May (Independence Day) and also in mountain huts, where it is accompanied with currant syrup.

Christmas Eve specialities vary from region to region, but boiled cod, boiled rib of mutton (*pinnekjøtt*), cod steeped in lye (*lutefisk*) and pork ribs (*ribbe*) are popular.

Drinks

A hearty meal should be washed down with beer and *akevitt* and then rounded off with cream cakes and coffee with brandy. While on the subject of drinks, the Vikings knew a lot about brewing beer and there are many different regional variations, including the celebrated Arctic Ale brewed by the Mack Brewery in Tromsø. *Akevitt*, Norway's most important alcoholic export and the country's only spirit, is sent across the equator on boats to mature, according to its traditional method of production, but is always served cold with simple fare. Spirits are subject to strict state control but are available at most restaurants and at the Vinmonopolet, the state-run retail outlet for alcohol, which is very expensive.

Finnebiff is usually served with boiled potatoes and cranberries. If you finish off with cloudberry ice cream made with fruit from the Norwegian uplands, you will have sampled a thoroughly Norwegian meal.

Restaurant selection

The following suggestions for Norway's main towns are listed according to four categories:
€€€€ = very expensive;
€€€ = expensive;
€€ = moderate;
€ = inexpensive.

Bergen

Enhjørningen, Bryggen, tel: 55 32 79 19. Famous fish restaurant in old wharfhouse. €€
Kafe Krystall, Kong Oscarsgate 16, tel: 55 32 10 84. Just minutes from the fish market, this intimate restaurant has only six tables and makes you feel like you are dining in the home of an elegant aunt. Menu changes daily. €€
Munkestuen Café, Klostergaten 12, tel: 55 90 21 49. Table reservation required at the weekend. Fifteen seats, a small menu, but the reputation of its cuisine and wine cellar goes beyond national boundaries. €€€
Ned's, Zachariasbryggen, tel: 55 55 96 55. Excellent seafood in an intimate waterfront setting. €€€
To Kokker (Two chefs), Bryggen, tel: 55 32 28 16. Located on the famous Bryggen in Bergen, this restaurant's specialities are game, fish and seafood.

Pubs include the **Portofino** in Hotel Bristol (Torgallmenning) and **The English Pub** (Ole Bulls plass 3), near the theatre. Both serve good beer in a typical Bergen atmosphere.

Kristiansand

Fish Restaurant Smia, Fosnagaten 30B, tel: 71 67 11 70. Fish prepared in many ways, with good service. Meat dishes also available. In an old sea house dating from 1787, with a good atmosphere. €€
Restaurant Bakgården, Tollbodgata 5, tel: 38 02 79 55. Fine French and international cuisine in an informal setting. €€
Sjøsterna, Skolegate 8, tel: 71 67 87 78. Intimate fish restaurant in the heart of the city. *Klippfisk*, a Norwegian variation of *bacalau* (dried cod) is a speciality. €€

Oslo

Bagatelle, Bygdøy Allé 3, tel: 22 12 14 40. This culinary institution has two Michelin stars. €€€€
Engebret Café, Bankplassen 1, tel: 22 82 25 25. Oldest restaurant in the city. Specialities: game and fish, and a lunchtime buffet. €€€
Grand Café, in the elegant Grand Hotel, Karl Johansgate 31, tel: 23 21 20 00. This elegant and traditional café was once frequented by Henrik Ibsen. €€€

Lofoten Fiskerestaurant, Stranden 75, Aker Brygge, tel: 22 83 08 08. Maritime atmosphere and excellent fish dishes. €€€

Magma, Bygdøy Allé 53, tel: 23 08 58 10. Opened in April 2000. Sonia Lee and her partner Laurent Sur-Nille worked with Alain Ducasse before launching Damien Hirst's restaurant in London. Very popular, so book in advance. €€€€

Punjab Sweet House, Grønland 24, tel: 22 17 20 86. For a change in flavours, try unpretentious Indian cooking in Oslo's immigrant area. Lamb curry and chicken tikka are some of the options available. €

Sult, Thorvald Meyers Gate 26, tel: 22 87 04 67. Specialising in 'new Norwegian' cuisine, this hip canteen has fresh seafood as the speciality; cooked any way you prefer. €€

Theatrecafeen, Hotel Continental, Stortingsgate 24, tel: 22 82 40 40. A famouse Viennese-style café. €€€

Pubs are situated in the streets off Karl Johans gate. **Smuget** (Rosenkrantzgate 22, tel: 22 42 52 62) is good on weekdays, otherwise try **Café Amsterdam** in Universitetsgata 11, a replica of a Dutch brown café. If the weather's fine and you want a drink outside, **Sara's Telt**, just off Karl Johans gate, is a good place to go.

Trondheim

Benitos mat-og vinhus, Vår Frues strete, tel: 73 52 64 22. Italian restaurant located in one of the riverside warehouses by the Nidelv. €€

Dromedar, Nedre Bakklandet 3A, tel: 73 50 25 15. Trendy yet relaxed café-bar by the river. €

Havfruen, Kjøppmannsgata 7, tel: 73 87 40 70. Delicious fish dishes and a classy atmosphere in an 18th-century wharf warehouse by the river. €€

Tromsø

Arctandria Restaurant, Strandtorget 1, tel: 77 60 07 25. *The* fish restaurant in Tromsø, with a great maritime atmosphere. Close to the harbour. Arctic specialities served on two floors; open for lunch and dinner. €€€

Aunegården, Sjøgata 29, tel: 77 65 12 34. Unique building with separate rooms, one which is cave-like. International menu and a lively crowd. €€

Brankos mat og vinhus, Storgata 57, tel: 77 68 26 73. Very good meat dishes and friendly service. A popular spot. Table reservations are advisable at the weekend. €€€

Compagniet Restauration, Sjøgata 12, tel: 77 66 42 22. Exclusive address for serious 4–5 course dining. €€€€

Theatrecafeen, Oslo

ACTIVE HOLIDAYS

According to the caricature, the ruck-sack is one of Norway's symbols, Norwegians are born with skis attached to their feet, and sweating it out in the open air is their favourite pursuit. But then they do have their own word for it: *friluftsliv* (life in the open air). This is a subject at primary school, and by the age of 16 everyone will have learnt the nine mountain rules, how to light a fire and how to survive outdoors. The days when a holidaymaker in Norway set off on his or her own with an inaccurate map are over. The tourist board has discovered that it is not just the Norwegians who want to commune with nature, so in recent years there has been a great expansion in the range of organised cycle, hiking and boat trips available.

HIKING AND GLACIER WALKING

Friluftsliv involves immersion in the great outdoors, and any tourist can share the experience as long as they have a good pair of walking shoes and the desire to learn. You can choose either to carry your own tent, stay in youth and family hostels, or ramble from cabin to cabin.

The most popular areas include the Jotenheim mountain range, the Rondane and Dovrefjell, the Hard-angervidda, the Telemark and the Finnmarksvidda. But a historic walk along the 'Rock-carving tour', through the very un-Norwegian landscape in the Østfold region to the southeast of Oslo, is also a rewarding experience. Hikers in the Dovrefjell can follow the King's Path all the way up to Trondheim. This route was followed by Catholic kings and pilgrims on their way to the cathedral city.

Tours on foot (or by bike) through the industrial regions can also be fun.

When railway lines, roads or hydro-electric power stations were built, it was often necessary to blast cuttings in the west Norwegian mountains, where thousands of migrant workers laboured with hammers and spades.

Such routes will interest anyone who enjoys energetic activities, has a love of history and appreciates the natural world, but it is definitely advisable to seek information beforehand as not all of them are danger-free. Some of the most scenic and interesting sections are situated in the Ryfylke region, southeast of Stavanger, and along the Bergen railway between Myrdal and Finse on the northern side of the Hardangerjøkulen glacier.

The Hardangerjøkulen, the Jostedalsbreen and the Svartisen in the far

Mountain survival

Hiking in the mountains is a serious and potentially dangerous business. Here are nine rules to observe to keep you safe.

1 Do not set out on a long walk unless you know you are physically fit.
2 Tell someone where you are going.
3 Respect the weather and check the weather forecast.
4 Take the advice of experienced hikers.
5 Be prepared for bad weather, even on a short walk. You should always carry a rucksack containing basic equipment with you when you are up in the mountains.
6 Do not forget your map and compass.
7 Never walk alone.
8 Turn back in good time if necessary. Do not be embarrassed about turning back.
9 Conserve your energy. If necessary, dig yourself into the snow. A spade is an extremely useful piece of equipment in the mountains, and you should always carry one with you.

north are bcoming increasingly popular with glacier walkers. Bear in mind, however, that you should never go onto a glacier without a local guide.

The Norwegian Tourist Board's *Mountain Hiking in Norway* gives details of route suggestions and other helpful advice, or you can contact the **Norwegian Mountain Touring Association (DNT)**, P.O. Box 8885 Youngstorget, 0028 Oslo, tel: 23 21 45 70, fax: 23 21 45 50, www.dnt.no

Winter wonderland

Snowmobile trips to the North Cape, reindeer safaris, dog-sled races and also horse-drawn sleigh rides are just some of the more unusual attractions of winter. You can also try your hand at ice fishing. Contact the tourist board for further information.

CLIMBING

Norway attracts mountaineers from all over Europe. Like walking and skiing, it is important to remember that the best gear in the world will count for nothing if the weather suddenly changes or if you have insufficient local knowledge to be able to find your way to a mountain hut or a farmhouse. Popular and challenging areas for climbers include the Lofoten and Vesterålen mountains, the Romsdalen valley, the Sunnmøre Alps and the Lyngen peninsula.

If you fancy a climb up a 2,000m (6,000ft) peak in the Jotunheimen National Park, then contact the nearest Norwegian tourist office *(see page 118)* for detailed information.

SKIING

Although Norway is first and foremost a walker's paradise – whether on foot or on skis – the range of Alpine sports is also wide. Geilo, Hemsedal, Lillehammer and Trysil in middle Norway and Narvik in the north have internationally renowned pistes. The best time of year for cross-country skiing is from February to April, when the sun is beginning to warm up and the streams are slowly coming back to life. The mountain scenery is then at its prettiest and the air at its clearest.

If you take a ski tour almost anywhere in Norway, then it is possible to spend a night in one of the DNT's mountain huts. While the socks, shoes and anoraks warm through in the drying cellar, exhausted skiing enthusiasts from all over the world can sit together beside the fireplace and fill up on generous portions of homemade food and enjoy a glass of wine.

Sledging tours are becoming increasingly popular. For further information on tour operators and resorts, contact the Norwegian Tourist Board *(see page 118)*. For the latest ski conditions, visit www.skiinfo.no

FISHING

The term 'coastal culture' has recently been coined by the Norwegians. What is meant by this is a combination of sporting activities and the absorption of the traditional maritime culture. Old fishermen's cabins *(rorbuer)* have opened up, and a type of holiday that even until the 1980s was restricted to the Lofoten Islands has spread to western Norway. The stronger the smell of fish, the more culture is imbibed.

Taking a trip on a fishing boat is all part of the experience, and if a 5kg (11lb) cod takes the bait in a Force Six sea, it will surely count as an unforgettable moment for any landlubber.

All anglers know that cod, coley and mackerel swim off the Norwegian coast. While fishing in the sea or in the fjords is free of charge, if you want to fish any of the inland waters, not to mention the exclusive salmon grounds, then you must buy a fishing licence from the post office and also a rod licence from the relevant landowner. However, it is debatable whether the expenditure will prove worthwhile in terms of catch weight.

Angling in Norway, published by the Norwegian Tourist Board, is a comprehensive guide to the best places to fish. The tourist board can also give you further information about rules and regulations *(see page 118)*.

Sailing, Canoeing and Rafting

Numerous rivers and lakes make Norway an ideal holiday destination for those interested in canoeing and kayaking. Some of the best places for these activities are the Lake Femund area, Østfold, Aust- and Vest-Agder, Telemark and suburban Oslo.

Canoeists and sailors head for the southern Norwegian coast and the fjords of western Norway, while divers prefer to search wrecks and look for treasure in the area around Oslofjord, Ålesund and Kristiansund.

White-water rides are not restricted to rip-roaring rivers with narrow gorges. On the Westfjord between Lofoten and the mainland, it is possible to try deep-sea rafting. If the wind and the currents are right, this is an experience that compares with the white waters on the River Sjoa in northern Gudbrandsdal.

Canoeists and rafters should contact the **Norwegian Canoe Association** for a list of organisers: Ullevaal Stadium, N-0840 Oslo, tel: 21 02 98 35, fax: 21 02 98 36, www.padling.no

Bird-Watching

The largest bird sanctuaries are in the Lofoten Islands, home to the black guillemot, cormorant, puffin, white-tailed eagle, kittiwake, fulmar, gannet and black-tailed godwit.

Another place for bird-watchers to head for is the Fokstumyra marsh, close to Dombås in eastern Norway, where no fewer than 87 species have been spotted.

The island of Runde, just off the coast near Ålesund, is famous as a nesting ground for more than half a million sea birds. The Rundebranden, the largest rock, lies within walking distance of Gøksoyr. The most common species are the kittiwake and puffin, but you will also find the razorbill, guillemot, fulmar, curlew, oyster catcher, eider and shellduck. If you are lucky, you might also see the white-tailed eagle, peregrine falcon, eagle owl or golden eagle.

White-water rafting

PRACTICAL INFORMATION

Getting There

BY SEA

Regular car ferries between Newcastle-upon-Tyne and sites on the west coast of Norway are operated both by **Fjord Line** and **DFDS Seaways**. Fjord Line travel three times a week in high season from Newcastle to Stavanger, Haugesund and Bergen and twice a week in low season. The crossing time is roughly 25 hours and boats travel for most of the year except for a couple of weeks in the winter. Contact Fjord Line at: Royal Quays, North Shields, Tyne and Wear, NE29 6EG, tel: 0870 143 9669, fjordline.uk@fjordline.com; www.fjordline.co.uk

DFDS operates an 18-hour service between Newcastle and Kristiansand, which then goes on to Gothenburg (26 hours); this runs from February to December, with two sailings per week. For further information, contact DFDS at Scandinavia House, Parkeston, Harwich, Essex, CO12 4QG, tel: 08705-444 333, www.dfdsseaways.co.uk

Smyril Line operates a weekly service from mid-May to September between Shetland and Bergen, with a crossing time of 13½ hours. The car ferry leaves Shetland at 10.30pm on Monday and arrives in Bergen at noon on Tuesday. The company will book your crossing from Aberdeen to Shetland for you, which is on P&O Scottish Ferries. For further details contact: Smyril Line, tel: 01595-690 845, fax: 01595-692 287; office@smyril-line.co.uk; www.smyril-line.com

BY AIR

From London Heathrow, **SAS Scandinavian Airlines** offers daily non-stop flights to Oslo and Stavanger (weekdays only). SAS also operates a service from Manchester to Oslo via Copenhagen, at least twice daily. For further information, contact: SAS Scandinavian Airlines, World Business Centre, Newall Road, London Heathrow, Hounslow, Middlesex, TW6 2RE, tel: 0845-607 2772, fax: 020-8990 7159, www.sas.no

British Airways offers up to five flights a day from London Heathrow to Oslo, tel: 0870-850 9850, www.ba.com; **Norwegian.no** (tel: 815 21 815, www.norwegian.no) operates daily from eight airports in Norway, in addition to flights from Oslo to London Stansted and southern Europe.

Cheap flights are offered by the no-frills airline **Ryanair**, which goes once a day from Liverpool and Newcastle and twice daily from London Stansted to Oslo Torp airport at Sandefjord, 130km (80 miles) south of the capital. Buses transport visitors into Oslo. For details call 0906-270 5656, www.ryanair.com. **Wideroe** (tel: 81 00 12 00, www.wideroe.no) has flights to Manchester, Aberdeen, Newcastle, Copenhagen, Gothenburg and Stockholm. It is based at Oslo Torp airport.

Most large North American cities have direct flights to Oslo on either American or European airlines.

Getting Around

BY CAR

Countless new roads have been built in recent years, old routes have been widened and sharp bends replaced with tunnels. But one still has to contend with the weather. In the south, west and east, the roads are clear of snow by the beginning of May, but potholes and bumps caused by frost and damage from snow chains linger into the summer. In the north and in the southern mountains snow can fall at the beginning of June. Those who plan to drive over the mountains in the autumn, winter or spring would be well advised to check that mountain passes are open, and ensure they are well equipped in case of break down or other emergency. Cars should use special winter tyres in snow conditions.

Tolls are often payable for entering into a city and for by-passes, long tunnels, bridges and some mountain passes.

Rules of the Road

The roads in Norway are generally good but some 'give way' rules can be confusing. As in all continental countries, vehicles drive on the right. If you're at the wheel, bear the following in mind:

• The speed limit on Norwegian motorways and some other main roads is 90kmph (56mph), but generally the top speed outside built-up areas is 80kmph (50mph). Exceed the speed limit and you can expect a very heavy fine.

• It is obligatory to drive all vehicles with dipped headlights on, even during the daytime.

• With an alcohol limit for drivers of 0.02 per-cent, it is better not to drink at all if driving.

• Fines are very high.

CARAVANS AND MOTOR HOMES

Many visitors prefer to bring their accommodation with them, making their holiday more affordable, and enabling travel further afield. While the advantages are clear, there is a down side. Traffic volume is increasing, car parks and lay-bys which were not meant for overnight stays now fill up with motor homes and caravans. Official rest stops and emptying sites for toilets are marked on the *Norway Camping* map available from the Norwegain Tourist Board *(see page 118)*. The maximum speed limit anywhere for vehicles towing trailers or caravans is 80kmph (50mph).

BY FERRY

Norway's long coastline means that taking the boat is often the quickest way of getting around; in the fjord area it is unavoidable. These ferries and express boats/catamarans operate from early in the morning until late at night. All vehicles under 5m (16ft) pay the same price. Cyclists and pedestrians can travel very cheaply on ferries.

The Coastal Express **Hurtigruten** sails up the coast of Norway all the way from Bergen to Kirkenes, covering a distance of 2,500 nautical miles. The service has been in operation for over 100 years, and for many coastal communities it was once the only link with the outside world, bringing not only visitors but also mail and vital provisions. Today, the journey is often described as the most picturesque cruise in the world. Passing through open sea and narrow sounds, it provides (weather permitting) magnificent views of some dramatic coastal scenery, including the impressive peaks of Helgeland and the 'Lofoten wall'.

Calling at 34 ports en route, the trip takes 11 days and 10 nights, but 'mini coastal voyages' or half round trips are possible. One can also stop off, explore the coastal region and then pick up the ferry the next day. If you are planning this sort of holiday, then make sure you book well in advance, particularly if travelling in June. There is space for up to 60 cars on the newer boats and the fares are certainly not cheap, but there is no need to book a cabin for short journeys and you can take your own meals in your rucksack.

BY RAIL

Norwegian State Railways (NSB) has a well developed network, connecting cities in the east, south, west and north. For details, including timetables and information on special tourist routes, visit www.nsb.no. Note that reservations are essential on Signatur trains. All the main lines have their own names with the *Bergensbanen* between Oslo and Bergen one of the most scenic, but the *Sørlandsbanen* from Oslo to Stavanger via Kristiansand, the *Dovrebanen* from Oslo to Trondheim, and the *Nordlandsbanen* from Trondheim to Fauske/Bodø are all worth exploring. Apart from the two northbound lines, none of these routes are connected. Particularly spectacular routes to recommend are the Flåm railway (branch line from the Bergen line, *see page 74*) and the *Raumabanen* from Dombås to Åndalsnes. If you plan to be travelling on several routes, the Scanrail Pass is good value.

BY BUS

In the north of Norway, you are dependent on buses and planes unless you have your own transport, but public transport can be a good option. The three-day bus journey from Fauske to Kirkenes is ideal for admiring the north Norwegian scenery, and it gives you the chance to stop off wherever you wish. The buses only run in the daytime with the three main sections as follows: Fauske–Narvik (5 hours), Narvik–Alta (11 hours) and Alta–Kirkenes (10 hours). Usually it is not necessary to pay in advance.

NOR-WAY **Bussekspress** (bus pass) guarantees a seat for all passengers. Before leaving home, visitors should enquire at their travel agent about purchasing the pass.

BY PLANE

Norway is exceptionally well served by the domestic airlines, making even the far north just a quick jaunt away. There are about 50 airports and airfields, including five on the Lofoten and Vesterålen islands alone.

Facts for the Visitor

TRAVEL DOCUMENTS

UK, US, Canadian and Australian citizens need only a passport for anything up to a three-month stay. Other nationals should contact their nearest Norwegian embassy for information on visa requirements.

CUSTOMS

Permitted imports for people aged 20 and over: 1 litre of spirits (up to 60 percent) plus 1 litre of fortified wine (up to 22 percent) or 2 litres wine (if no spirits), and 2 litres of beer plus 200 cigarettes. Only tinned and bottled food products may be imported apart from

The train is a great way to travel

3kg (7lbs) of fresh meat, which must be stamped in the country of origin.

TOURIST INFORMATION

The **Norwegian Tourist Board** provides excellent general tourist material on Norway and its various regions. It cannot, however, book tickets or accommodation.

In the UK: Norwegian Tourist Board, Charles House, 5 Lower Regent Street, London SW1Y 4LR, tel: 020 7839 6255 or 0906-302 2003 (24-hour brochure hotline); fax: 020-7839 6014, www.visit.norway.com

In the US: Norwegian Tourist Board, 655 Third Avenue, New York, NY 10017, tel: 212 885 9700, fax: 212 885 9710.

IN NORWAY:

The **Norway Information Centre** in Oslo provides information about Oslo and the rest of Norway: Tourist Information by the City Hall, Fridtjof Nansens Plass 5, N-0160 Oslo, tel: 24 14 77 00, fax: 22 42 92 22, e-mail: info@visitoslo.com; www.visitnorway.com

In addition to the main regional tourist offices, there are around 350 **tourist information offices**, which provide visitors with informative

material and advice and book accommodation or transport. Here are the main ones:

Ålesund: Keiser Wilhelms Gate 11, N-6003 Ålesund, tel: 70 15 76 00.
Balestrand: N-6898 Balestrand, tel: 57 69 16 17.
Bergen: Vågsallmenningen 1, N-5003 Bergen, tel: 55 55 20 00.
Brønnøysund: N-8901 Brønnøysund, tel: 75 01 12 10.
Fredrikstad: Tøihusgata 41, N-1632 Gamle Fredrikstad, tel: 69 30 46 00.
Hamar: Vikingskipet, N-2321 Hamar; P.O. Box 560, N-2304 Hamar, tel: 62 51 75 03.
Kongsberg: Karsches gate 3, N-3611 Kongsberg, tel: 32 73 50 00.
Kristiansand: Kirkegata 15, N-4611 Kristiansand S; P.O. Box 633, N-4665 Kristiansand S, tel: 38 02 52 63.
Lillehammer: Jernbanetorget 2, N-2609 Lillehammer; P.O. Box 44, N-2601 Lillehammer, tel: 61 28 98 00.
Molde: Turistinformasjonen, in Molde town hall, tel: 71 25 71 33.
Narvik: Kongensgate 66, N-8500 Narvik, tel: 76 94 33 09.
Oslo: Fridtjof Nansens Plass 5, N-0160 Oslo, tel: 24 14 77 00.
Rjukan: Rjukan turistkontor, Torget 2, N-3660 Rjukan, tel: 35 09 12 90.
Røros: Peder Hiortsgate 2, N-7460 Røros, tel: 72 41 11 65.

Street life, Aker Brygge

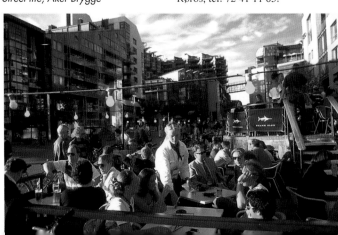

Websites at a glance
This is a selection of the many sites on the web. Each has a 'www.' prefix.

visitbergen.com	*Bergen site*
bike-norway.com	*cycling in Norway*
destinasjontromso.no	*Tromsø site*
fjordnorway.no	*details on the fjords*
flaamsbana.no	*all about the Flåm railway*
hardangerfjord.com	*Hardanger and its fjords*
sorlandet.com	*Kristiansand site*
museumsnett.no	*for Norway's museums*
norlandia.no	*hotels on-line*
norway.org.uk	*Norwegian government site*
trondheim.com	*Trondheim*
trondelag.com	*central Norway*
visitnorway.com	*offical Norwegian Tourist Board site*
visitoslo.com	*all about the capital*

Skien: Nedre Hjellegate 18, N-3724 Skien, tel: 35 90 55 20.
Stavanger: Rosenkildetorget 1, N-4001 Stavanger, tel: 51 85 92 00.
Svolvær: Torget 21, N-8300, Svolvær, tel: 76 06 98 00.
Tromsø: Storgata 61, N-9008 Tromsø, tel: 77 61 00 00.
Trondheim: Aktivum AS, Munkegata 19, N-7013 Trondheim, tel: 73 80 76 62.
Tvedestrand: Fritz Smiths Gate 1, N-4900, Tvedestrand, tel: 37 16 11 01.
Vardø: Kaigata 8, N-9950 Vardø, tel: 78 98 69 07.
Voss: Uttrågata 9, N-5700 Voss, tel: 56 52 08 00.

CURRENCY AND EXCHANGE

The Norwegian unit of currency is the kroner (NOK, about 12 to £1, seven to US$1), which comprises 100 øre. There are notes to the value of 1,000, 500, 100 and 50 kroner, plus 20, 10, 5, 1 krone and 50 øre coins. Credit cards including Visa, MasterCard and Cir-

rus are widely accepted. Travellers can bring in money (Norwegian and foreign) up to the value of 25,000 kroner.

OPENING TIMES

Most shops are open from at least 10am–5pm; many stay open until 8pm, particularly on Thursdays. Banks open weekdays from 8.30am until 3.30pm (3pm in summer), and 5pm on Thursday.

PUBLIC HOLIDAYS

New Year's Day, Maundy Thursday, Good Friday, Easter Monday, 1 May, 17 May (Independence Day), Ascension Day, Whit Monday, Christmas Day and Boxing Day.

SOUVENIRS

Popular souvenirs include knitwear, glass, pewter, silver jewellery, trolls, carved wooden goods and pottery.

TAX-FREE SHOPPING

If your purchase exceeds NOK 308, the store should issue you with a tax-free receipt for the amount of VAT paid. On departure from Norway, a refund of 11–18 percent will be given to you on presentation of goods, tax-free receipt and passport, as long as the item has not been used in Norway. Look out for tax-free representatives at airports/ports.

POSTAL SERVICES

Most post offices are open Monday to Friday 9am–5pm and Saturday until 1pm.

TELEPHONE

Phone cards are available from 'Narvesen' kiosks and post offices. Cheap international phone cards are available at other local kiosks. Coin phones accept 1, 5, 10 and 20 kroner coins. Some phones take credit cards. To call abroad from Norway, dial the

> ### The midnight sun
> The best time to see the midnight sun in northern Norway is in high summer. The sun does not sink below the horizon at the North Cape from the second week in May to the last week in July. What you lose in the winter darkness is made up for many times over in the surprising summer months. The best chance of seeing the Northern Lights is between November and February, from north of the Arctic Circle. This magical, unexpected light show is never the same. The *aurora borealis* shimmers in shades of blue and violet dancing across the sky, like some heavenly symphony.

international code (00), then the country code: UK 44; US/Canada 1. Leave out the initial zero of the local code when calling the UK. To call Norway from abroad, dial 0047 then the number. All Norwegian telephone numbers have eight digits. There are no local codes.

TIME
Norway is one hour ahead of Greenwich Mean Time (GMT); 6 hours ahead of Eastern Standard Time.

VOLTAGE
220 volts AC. UK visitors should bring an adaptor with two round-ended prongs; US visitors require a transformer.

DISABLED
A growing number of hotels and campsites are adapting their facilities for people with disabilities. The Norwegian State Railways provide special facilities for disabled travellers, and the new Coastal Express ships have good facilities for wheelchair users including elevators and cabins. Details are available from the Norwegian Tourist Board. There are also coach tours around Norway especially for wheelchair users. Contact: Euro Terra Nova AS, Møllergata 4, N-0179 Oslo, tel: 22 94 13 50.

MEDICAL
In the event of illness or injury, visit a doctor's surgery *(legevakt)* first. Norway being an EEA member (European Economic Agreement) entitles all visitors from other member countries to the same basic medical rights as a Norwegian citizen provided they have the necessary documentation (Form E111). It is, however, advisable to have some form of medical travel insurance.

EMERGENCIES
In an emergency in Norway, dial: **110** (Fire Service); **112** (Police Service); **113** (Ambulance Service).

TAXIS
Taxis are plentiful in the towns, but expensive. An extra 35 percent is payable on Sundays and holidays. Take a taxi from a rank or else order one by phone (tel: 02323).

WHAT TO WEAR
Even if visiting Norway in the summer, pack clothes for all seasons. Walkers should be prepared for the cold and the rain.

ALCOHOL
Alcoholic drinks are very expensive in Norway. Wines and spirits are only sold in the Vinmonopolet shops, which are in most larger towns.

SMOKING
Smoking is not permitted on any means of public transport (except on special carriages on the Norwegian State Railway) or in public buildings and eating and drinking venues, such as restaurants and pubs.

ACCOMMODATION

CAMPING

Most Norwegian holiday makers take their homes with them. Motor homes and caravans are much more in evidence than tents, but campsites are preferable to car-parks or lay-bys for an overnight stay. The standard of the 1,400 sites is high. Stars are used to give guidance on the facilities available, but even the cheapest campsites have basic sanitary installations, and prices on the best sites are not astronomical. Many campsites are, however, squeezed between a river and a road. If you intend to stay put for a few days, it is better to try to find a site in a quieter spot – they are usually well signposted.

There is one other possibility: the Norwegian *allemannsrett* permits the erection of a tent away from an official camp-site as long as it is not closer than 150m (160yds) to a house or similar accommodation and is on land that is not used for agricultural purposes. Every Norwegian is aware of this right and, provided that locals and tourists abide by the accompanying rules, *camping sauvage* in Norway will continue to be allowed.

Many campsites have cabins that can usually be booked in advance. The cabins are classified and given one–five stars depending on their size and standard. The smaller and simpler they are, the cheaper they will be, but expect to find bunk beds, basic wooden furniture, old-fashioned equipment with a hot-plate, wall heating and a toilet within sight. For many people, this is ideal. After a long walk in the rain, a cabin is certainly far preferable to the limitations of a tent.

The *Norway Camping Guide*, including a list of all official campsites, is available from the Norwegian Tourist Board or The Norwegian Hospitality Association (RBL), Essendropsgata 6, N-0305 Oslo, tel: 22 02 76 00, fax: 23 08 86 21. Check out also www.camping.no

SELF-CATERING CHALETS AND CABINS

Called *hytte* in Norwegian, this type of accommodation is perfect for those who prefer to explore one part of the country thoroughly. Rather like British country cottages, *hytter* come in various

A hytte is a good place to stay

sizes, but they normally house four to six people. They always have the full basic equipment, and furnishings range from the simply comfortable to the sumptuous; prices vary accordingly. *Hytter* have to be rented by the week and advance booking is necessary.

Popular amongst hikers are the *fjell-stove* or *fjellstue*, a mixture between cabins and guesthouses, where you can stay the night and enjoy simple but delicious food.

The biggest chalet and cabin agency is **Novasol**, www.novasol.com, but the Norwegian Tourist Board has information (*see page 118*), as does Fjordhytter, who publish *Holiday Homes in Fjord Norway*, a catalogue featuring 1,000 well-equipped comfortable homes in beautiful settings. Also try www.norges booking.com for hytter.

👁 Coastal cabins

The cabins along the coast are called either *rorbuer* (fishermen's cabins) or *sjøhus* (sea cabins). Most of them are located by the quayside, and a boat, life jackets and fishing tackle are included. Watersports activities are usually a central element in a cabin holiday. These cabins used to be restricted to northern Norway – on Lofoten in particular – but are becoming more and more popular in the south and west of the country. Like the classical cabin holiday, this type of holiday accommodation is very much in the Norwegian tradition.

TOURIST HOTELS

Rural tourist hotels are usually in pleasant spots and are designed like villas. Prices are often surprisingly reasonable and it is well worth stopping and enquiring. Even if the rooms and furniture seem old and in need of renovation, the atmosphere is generally very warm and the other guests friendly. Details about hotels and the various hotel passes and discount schemes are available from the Norwegian Tourist Board (*see page 118*).

Hotel Selection

The following suggestions are listed according to three categories and are for two people in a double room with breakfast:

€€€ = expensive
€€ = moderate
€ = inexpensive

Ålesund

Comfort Home Hotel Bryggen, Apothekergate 1–3, N-6004 Ålesund, tel: 70 12 64 00, fax: 70 12 11 80, e-mail: bryggen@comfort.choice.no A stylishly restored warehouse by the waterfront in the picturesque harbour district. High standard of comfort with spacious rooms. €€

Balestrand

Kringsjå Hotell Vandrerheim, N-6899 Balestrand, tel: 57 69 13 03, fax: 57 69 16 70, e-mail: kringsja@kringsja.no, www.kringsja.no This former artist's villa has been modernised but still retains its distinctive character. Lovely views of the Sognefjord. Hotel and hostel accommodation; good-value restaurant and self-catering available. €

Kvikne's Hotel, N-6899 Balestrand, tel: 57 69 42 00, fax: 57 69 42 01, e-mail: booking@kviknes.no, www.kviknes.no Traditional Swiss-style hotel, once a favourite of Kaiser Wilhelm II. Sauna, gym, jacuzzi. €€–€€€

Beitostølen

Radisson SAS Resort Beito, N-2953 Beitstølen, tel: 61 35 30 00, fax: 61 35 30 01, e-mail: info.beitostolen@radissonsas.com, www.beitostolen.radissonsas.com Primarily a winter sports hotel. Distinctive and attractive timber style. €€€

Bergen

Best Western Victoria, Kong Oscargate 29, tel: 55 21 23 00, fax: 55 32 81 78. Once a staging-post inn, this (family-run) charming hotel has 43 simple rooms with their own facilities. Full of character, it also has an impressive collection of art. €€€

Clarion Admiral, C. Sundtsgate 9–13, tel: 55 23 64 00. One of Bergen's finest hotels with waterfront views and a superb restaurant. €€€

Crowded House, Håkonsgaten 27, tel: 55 90 72 00, fax: 55 23 13 30, e-mail: info@crowded-house.com Innovative pension/hostel with cheerful ambience and a hip café. €

First Hotel Marin, Rosenkrantzgaten 8, tel: 53 05 15 00, fax: 53 05 15 01, e-mail: booking.marin@firsthotels.no Stylish rustic design combined with all modern facilities. €€€

Grand Hotel Terminus, Zander Kaaesgaten 6, tel: 55 21 25 00, fax: 55 21 25 01, e-mail: booking@grand-hotel-terminus.no Elegant, old-world hostelry across from the railway station, and a 10 minute walk to centre. €€

Hotel Charm, Rosenbergsgaten 13, tel: 55 23 10 70, fax: 55 23 10 71. Centrally located. All rooms have bath, toilet, TV. €€

Hotel Park, Harald Hårfagresgate 35, N-5007 Bergen, tel: 55 54 44 00, fax: 55 54 44 00. One of the best pensions in town. Central location but in a quiet spot. Friendly staff. €€€

Brekke

Brekkestranda Fjord Hotell, N-5961 Brekke, tel: 57 78 55 00, fax: 57 78 56 00, e-mail: bstranda@online.no Unusual interior. All rooms have access to garden and a view of the fjord. €€

Brønnøysund

Torghatten Feriesenter & Hotell, N-8900 Brønnøysund, tel: 75 02 53 41, fax: 75 02 55 80. Modern hotel, good location, great view, spacious rooms and cabins. €€

Fedje

Kræmmerholmen, N-5133 Fedje, tel: 56 16 42 05, fax: 56 16 42 06. White cottages by the fjord, which date from 1700s. €€

Forvik

Handelstedet Forvik, N-8976 Velevstad, tel: 75 03 71 31, fax: 75 03 76 34. Established in 1792. Fine view over the fjord and the Seven Sisters. €€

Gudvangen

Gudvangen Hotell, tel: 57 63 39 29, fax: 57 63 39 80. Explore Sogn's many attractions under the shadow of majestic mountains and waterfalls. Well-located at a ferry point for Norway in a Nutshell travellers *(see page 74)*. Authentically furnished rooms. Good restaurant and cafeteria. €€

Hardangervidda

Halne Fjellstove, N-5785 Vøringsfoss, tel: 53 66 57 12, fax: 53 66 50 83. Apartments, rooms and comfortable cabins, hearty *Fjell* fare and information about walking tours. Closed in winter, opens at Easter. €€

Kongsberg

Gyldenløve, Hermann Vossgate 1, tel: 32 86 58 00, fax: 32 86 58 01. Large friendly hotel. Good for families. €€

Quality Grand Hotel, Kristian Augustsgate 2, N-3611, tel: 32 77 28 00, fax: 32 73 41 29. Comfortable hotel with friendly service. €€

Kristiansand

Rica Travel Hotel, Dronningensgate 66–68, N-4602 Kristiansand, tel: 38 02 15 00, fax: 38 02 01 19. Intimate atmosphere and attentive service, with a pleasant restaurant serving good meat dishes. €€€

Thon Hotel Welgeland, Kirkegaten 15, N-4611 Kristiansand, tel: 38 17 20 40, fax: 38 02 73 21. A hotel in the Thon chain in the town centre. Family atmosphere, with small rooms, excellent breakfasts and good Norwegian cooking. €€

Lofthus
Hotel Ullensvang, N-5787 Lofthus, tel: 53 67 00 00, fax: 53 67 00 01, www.hotel-ullensvang.no Nice, comfortable hotel with a range of sports activities and pools. €€–€€€

Molde
Tulip Inn Thon Hotel Knausen Panorama, N-6416 Molde, tel: 23 08 02 00, fax: 71 19 11 10, e-mail: knausen@rainbow-hotels.no 3km (2 miles) east of Molde. Airport bus stops outside this hotel, in the Rainbow chain, and run to a high standard. Very fine views of the Romsdalen mountains. €€–€€€

Morgedal
Morgedal Hotel, N-3848 Morgedal, tel: 35 06 89 00, fax: 35 06 89 01, e-mail: morgedal-hotell@kviteseid.online.no, www.morgedal.no Timber construction adds to the warm and welcoming atmosphere. Family-friendly, with high standards. €€–€€€

Mosjøen
Fru Haugans Hotel, Strandgate 39, N-8650 Mosjøen, tel: 75 11 41 00, fax: 75 11 41 01, www.fruhaugans.no Quiet and stylishly furnished. The restaurant serves tasty fish dishes. €€

North Cape (Nordkapp)
Nordkapp Turistheim, N-9763 Skarsvåg, tel/fax: 78 47 52 67. Basic standard. View out to sea. Serves excellent fish dishes. €€€

Oslo
Best Western Hotel Bondeheimen, Rosen-krantzgate 8, N-0159 Oslo, tel: 23 21 41 00, fax: 23 21 41 01, www.oslo-prp.no/ bondeheimen Central location and easy to find. One of the cheapest of the better class hotels, with a traditional atmosphere; the restaurant serves good Norwegian dishes. €€

Comfort Hotel Gabelshus, Gabelsgaten 16, tel: 23 27 65 00, fax: 23 27 65 60. An ivy-clad hotel with excellent service and a good traditional kitchen. Fireplace in lobby is cosy in cool months. €€

Continental, Stortingsgaten 24, tel: 22 82 40 00, fax: 22 42 96 89. Estab-

Grand Hotel, Oslo

lished in 1909 and still family-run. Where royalty and rock stars stay. Excellent restaurant, café and bar attract locals. €€€

Ellingsens Pensjonat, Holtegt., N-0355 Oslo, tel: 22 60 03 59, fax: 22 60 99 21. Central, but quiet location in an old villa surrounded by a pleasant garden. Close to the royal palace. €€

Grand Hotel, Karl Johans Gate 31, tel: 23 21 20 00, fax: 23 21 21 00, www.grand.no High level of comfort in one of the capital's long-standing institutions. Spacious and pleasant atmosphere, particularly in the lobby. Facilities include an indoor pool, sauna, health club and several restaurants. €€€

SAS Radisson Scandinavia Hotel, Holbergsgate 30, tel: 23 29 30 00, fax: 23 29 30 01. Oslo's only skyscraper remains visible from many points across the city. Popular among business clientele. Rooms in different styles. €€€

Rjukan

Rjukan Fjellstue, 3660 Rjukan, tel: fax: 35 09 51 62, in Skinnarbu 20km (12 miles) to the west. Log cabin style, rustic furniture, basic standard. Pure Telemark. €€

Rødberg

Rødberg Hotel, N-3630 Rødberg, tel: 32 74 16 40, fax: 32 74 13 81. Very comfortable with good service. Children not welcome. €€€

Røros

Quality Hotel & Resort Røros, An-Magrittsvei, N-7374 Røros, tel: 72 40 80 00, fax: 72 40 80 01. Traditional wooden guesthouse, comfortably furnished. €€

Stalheim

Stalheim Hotel, tel: 56 52 01 22, fax: 56 52 00 56, www.stalheim.com Dating to 1885, the original inn has a fascinat-

Hotel passes

There are several types of hotel pass available for people travelling through the country in the summer. The Norway Fjord Pass offers savings at more than 200 participating hotels, pensions, and mountain lodges (including breakfast) throughout Norway. One Fjord Pass is valid for two adults and their accompanying children under the age of 15, sharing the room. Advance reservations can be made through the central reservation office in Bergen. You pay the reduced rate directly to the hotel. Special children's rates are also available. The Nordic Hotel Pass and Scan+Hotel Pass are further variations of the scheme. For further information visit www.fjordpass.no

ing history. Family-run, the present hotel was built in 1960. The terrace offers magnificent views of surrounding valleys and waterfalls and mountain peaks. €€

Stavanger

Skagen Brygge Hotel, Skagenkaien 30, N-4004 Stavanger, tel: 51 85 00 00, fax: 51 85 00 01, e-mail: bryggeho@ online.no By the quay. Pleasant atmosphere. Fourteen good restaurants nearby. €€€ (€€ in July with special summer deals)

Svensby

Svensby Tursenter, N-9064 Svensby, tel: 77 71 22 25. Comfortable huts (55 sq m/600 sq ft each) and rooms close to Svensby ferry port at the Ullsfjord. €€

Tranøy

Tranøy Fyr, N-8297 Tranøy, tel: 913 28 013, www.tranoyfyr.no An old lighthouse with views of the Lofoten wall. €€€

Tromsø

Comfort Hotel Saga, Richard withs plass 2, tel: 77 60 70 00, fax: 77 60

70 10. Excellently located in an attractive central square. Decent restaurant. €€–€€€

Skipperhuset Pensjonat, Storgata 12, tel: 77 68 16 60, fax: 77 65 62 92. Centrally located; in a simple style, with an adjoining café. Little in the way of luxuries. €

Trondheim

Hotel Britannia, Dronningensgate 5, N-7001, tel: 73 80 08 00, fax: 73 80 08 01, e-mail: firmapost@britannia.no, www.britannia.com Luxury hotel in a central location. Offers reasonable prices to tourists with a hotel pass. €€€

Comfort Home Bakeriet Hotel, Brattørgata 2, tel: 73 99 10 00, fax: 73 99 10 01. Small and intimate. Prices include half board. €€

Thon Hotel Gildevangen, Søndregate 22b, tel: 23 08 02 00, fax: 23 08 02 90. Good-standard accommodation in this hotel in the trusty Rainbow chain. Tasty breakfasts, and extremely convenient for the railway station. €€

Trondheim Vandrerhjem Rosenborg, Weidemannsvei 41, tel: 73 87 44 50, fax: 73 87 44 55. Overnight accommodation in four- or six-bed rooms. €

Voss

Fleischer's Hotel, Evangervegen 13, tel: 56 52 05 00, fax: 56 52 05 01, www.fleischers.no Centrally located, this family-run, unusual looking hotel was built in 1899 and last renovated in 1997. Modern facilities with character. Swimming pool, sauna, tennis court and other facilities. €€€

Kringsjå Pensjonat, Strengjarhaugen 6, tel: 56 51 16 27, fax: 56 51 63 30. Central but still quiet, with a good standard of accommodation. €€

YOUTH HOSTELS

There are more than 100 *Vandrerhjem* or youth hostels in Norway, many of which make ideal starting points for walking tours. Offering a surprisingly high standard of accommodation at a reasonable price, they are open to anybody and are ideal for young people and families on a budget, though many are open only in summer, from June until the end of August.

Most hostels have living rooms to relax in, and the bedrooms normally have two, four or six beds. Some bedrooms have their own bathrooms. Many establishments serve hot food, and breakfast may be included in the price. Others are self-catering. All you need to take with you is a sheet sleeping bag. The hostels are awarded one to three stars, and prices vary considerably per person per night for Youth Hostel Association members, depending on category and type of room. Non-members pay a little more.

Other cheap hostel-style accommodation for backpack travellers is often available in towns, for example at the YMCA, but prices will vary.

For details on youth hostels it is advisable to contact your own national youth hostel headquarters or the following address in Norway: **Norske Vandrerhjem** (Hostelling International Norway), Torggata 1, N-0181 Oslo, tel: 23 13 93 00, fax: 23 13 93 50, e-mail: hostels@vandrerhjem.no Their booklet *Norske Vandrerhjem* gives details on hostels across Norway; they are popular, so booking in high season is essential.

INDEX